Knit Real Shetland

15 knitting projects in Real Shetland Wool from Jamieson & Smith

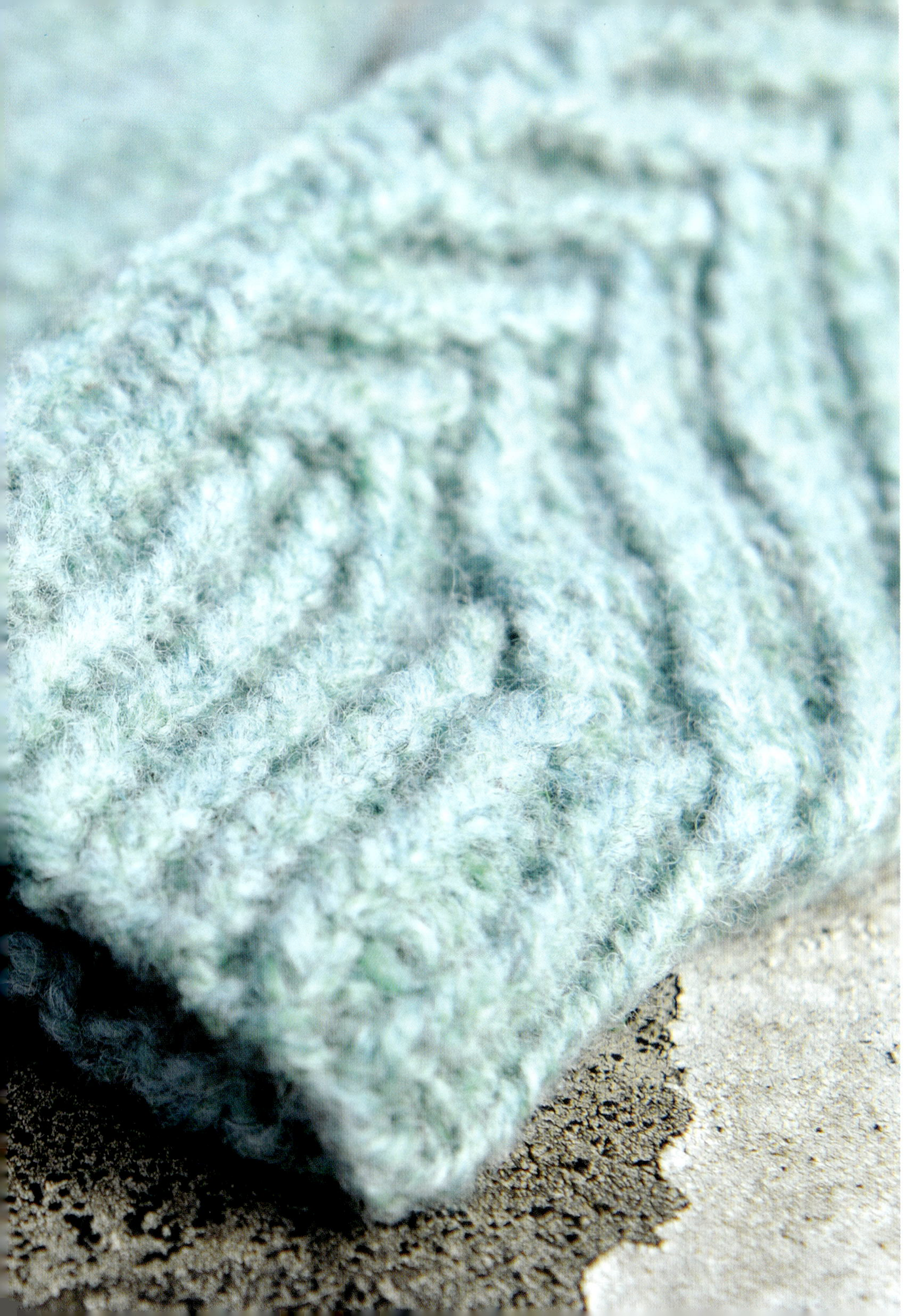

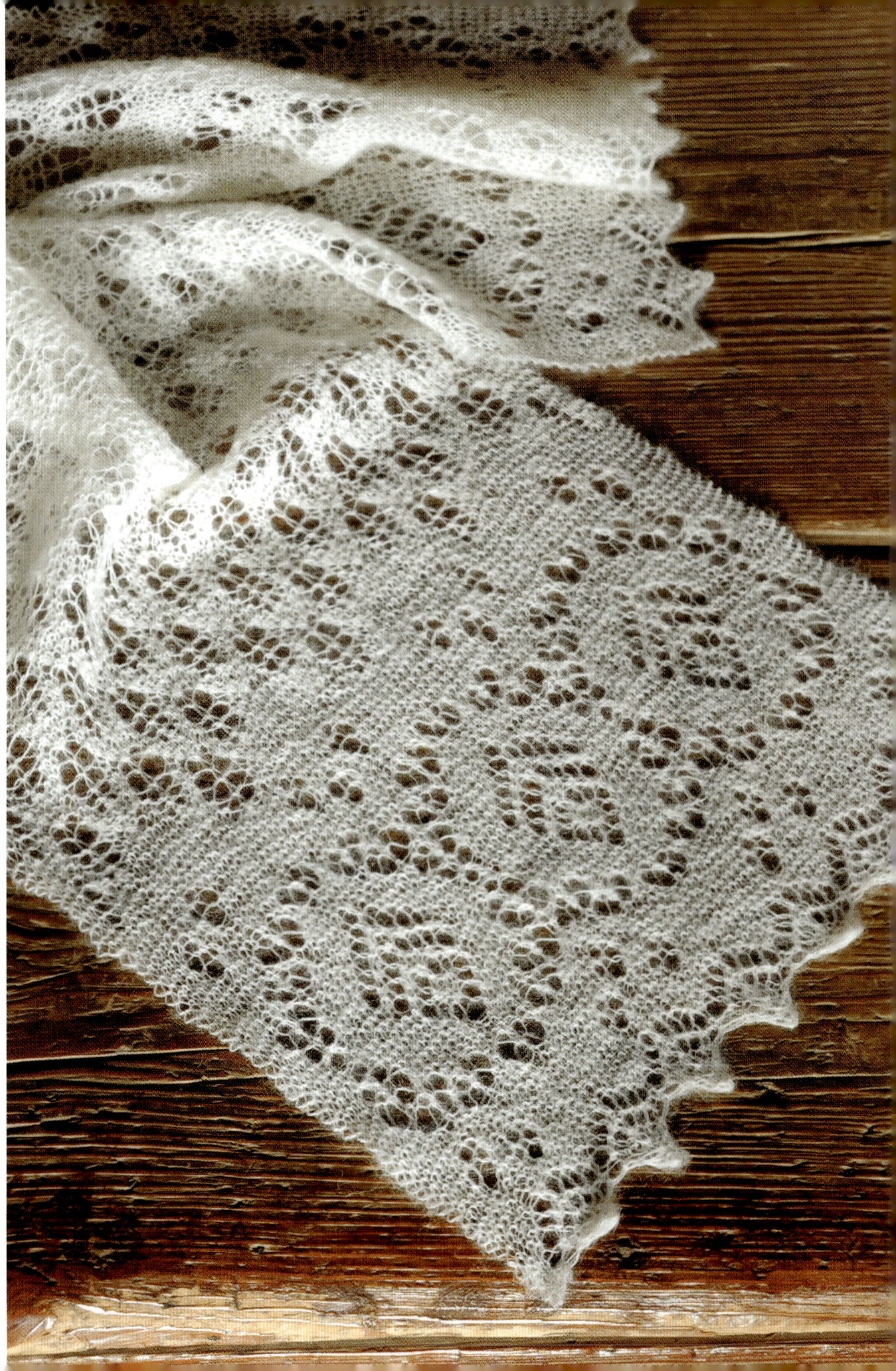

Knit Real Shetland

15 knitting projects in Real Shetland Wool from Jamieson & Smith

introduction by **Kate Davies**

published by **Jamieson & Smith Shetland Wool Brokers, Ltd.**

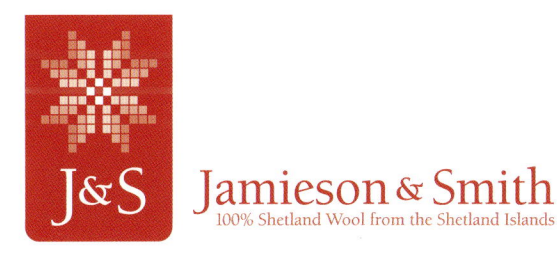

EDITOR
Sarah Laurenson

COVER AND INTERIOR DESIGN
Laura Palumbo

TECHNICAL EDITOR
Jen Arnall-Culliford

PHOTOGRAPHER
Dave Donaldson

Printed by Creative Colour Bureau, Glasgow, Scotland, United Kingdom.

Copyright © 2011 Jamieson & Smith Shetland Wool Brokers, Ltd.

All rights reserved. No part of this publication may be reproduced, stored in a retrieval system, or transmitted in any for or by any means, electronic, mechanical, photocopying, recording, or otherwise, with the prior permission of the copyright holder.

We give permission to readers to photocopy the instructions and graphics for personal use only.

ISBN 978-0-9570326-0-6 (paperback)
ISBN 978-0-9570326-1-3 (eBook)

Produced in Shetland by Jamieson & Smith Shetland Wool Brokers, Ltd.
90 North Road, Lerwick, ZE1 0PQ United Kingdom
01595 693 579 | info@jamiesonandsmith.co.uk

dedicated to our wool producers

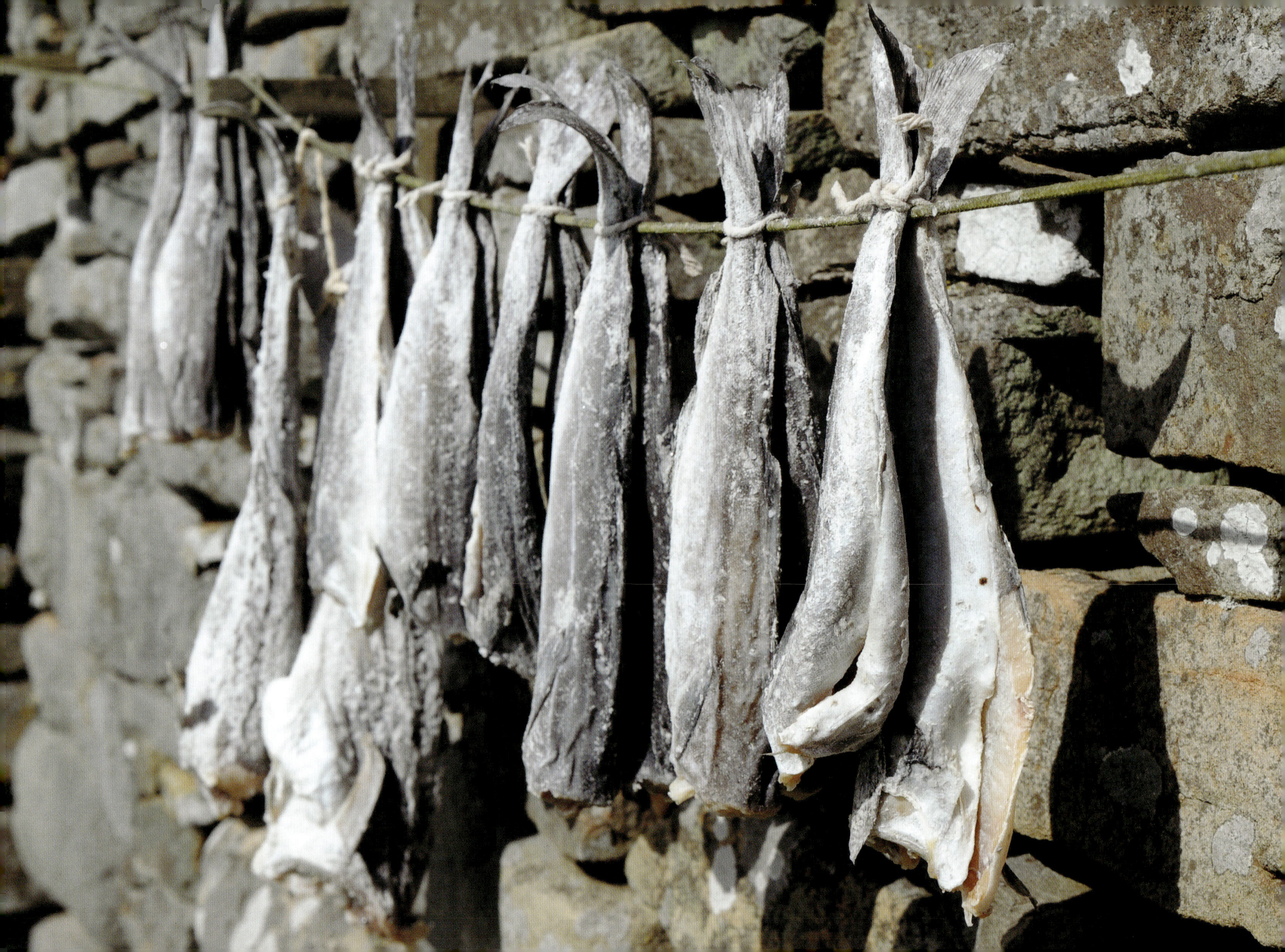

Table of Contents

Introduction .... page 8

Patterns

    Wave Cardigan *designed by Toshiyuki Shimada & Grace Williamson* .... page 10

    Feathercrest Mittens *designed by Jared Flood* .... page 16

    Peat Hill Waistcoat *designed by Hazel Tindall* .... page 20

    Cross Tam *designed by Daniel Goldman* .... page 26

    Viking Tunic *designed by Sandra Manson* .... page 30

    Osaka Tea Cosy *designed by Masami Yokoyama* .... page 34

    Kergord Scarf *designed by Mary Kay* .... page 38

    Melby Jumper Dress *designed by Gudrun Johnston* .... page 42

    Wool Brokers Socks *designed by Lesley Smith* .... page 46

    Muckleberry Gloves & Hat *designed by Mary Jane Mucklestone* .... page 50

    Caavie Gansey *designed by Candace Eisner Strick* .... page 54

    Madeira Lace Shawl *designed by Joyce Ward* .... page 60

    Buttoned Hat *designed by Woolly Wormhead* .... page 66

    Olly's Allover *designed by Jean Moss* .... page 70

Abbreviations .... page 76

Project Gallery .... page 77

Designer Biographies .... page 78

General Information .... page 79

Acknowledgements .... page 80

Eva Smith on the pony, with her father John Smith (Auld Sheepie), and a friend on the Shetland Ram. Berry Farm, c. 1935.
Photo courtesy of Shetland Museum and Archives.

Introduction

One fine summer morning in 1946, a truck set off from Berry Farm, Scalloway, with its driver, Magnie Halcrow, and a passenger, 15-year-old Eva Smith. It was Eva's school holidays, but she wasn't on a jaunt: her hands held a chequebook full of blank, signed cheques, and her head was full of pricing information.

Eva had a job to do. Her father, John, had sent her to the village of Walls on Shetland's West Mainland with instructions to buy wool. John was a livestock trader, an expert on his native Shetland Sheep and a skilled grader of fleeces; his nickname—Auld Sheepie—suggests the estimation in which his expertise was held. John had built up a reputation for sorting and grading during the 1930s and, by 1946, found himself in unprecedented demand. These were the years of the post-war knitwear boom and the industry placed high demands for uniformity on the producers of increasingly popular Shetland wool. From Berry Farm, John successfully graded fleeces for the consistency and quality the market required, then brokered the wool for processing and sale. By the late afternoon of that fine summer's day in 1946, Eva had finished her work, and, with the truck laden with fleeces, set off back to Scalloway. She didn't know it then but these were the beginnings of Jamieson & Smith Shetland Wool Brokers, which she would later run with her brother, Jim Smith (better known as Jim o' Berry).

By 1950, John had joined forces with James Jamieson and relocated the business to Lerwick. The pair began in a building behind Victoria Pier, and later moved to the company's present premises on North Road, giving easy access to the steamers that ran south to Leith and Aberdeen. North Road thus came to be associated with two distinctive Shetland industries: wool and herring.

In season, the area bustled with the itinerant men and women of the herring trade (the building that Jamieson & Smith now use as their yarn store in fact started life as a 'rest' for the gutter lassies who followed the Scottish fleet). These gutter lassies were enthusiastic knitters, keen to learn new patterns and techniques at the hands of Shetland's craftswomen, and eager to buy yarn from the conveniently placed brokers on North Road. When the herring moved on, so did the women, but they still needed good Shetland yarn to knit with. The Wool Brokers were happy to post packages South, and, spurred on by the custom of the gutter lassies, the mail-order side of Jamieson & Smith became increasingly important. While the market for raw Shetland wool fluctuated under competition from man-made fibres and the ubiquitous merino, demand for quality Shetland yarn—light, lofty, and ideally suited to fine lace and Fair Isle knitting—remained buoyant.

This two-pronged approach to selling Shetland wool—grading and brokerage on the one hand, yarn mail-order and marketing on the other—remained crucial to Jamieson & Smith's development through the 1960s and 70s. Sorting and grading (now in the capable hands of Oliver Henry who arrived for a summer job in 1967, and never left) meant that each fleece gave the most value that it could back to Shetland's economy, supporting local wool production, and encouraging the conservation of the native breed of sheep. Meanwhile, the marketing side of the business allowed Shetland's important hand-knitting traditions to reach a much wider audience, not only through Jamieson & Smith's quality yarns, but in the popular patterns the company commissioned from talented designers, such as Gladys Amedro and Mary Kay.

Shetland is the only place in the British Isles where domestic hand-knitting has thrived continuously from the seventeenth century to the present day. In a singular way, knitting is bound up with local culture, but a deep sense of tradition does not make the craft static or insular. From its beginnings, when canny crofters traded stockings with Dutch merchants, through to the beautiful Victorian lace produced in response to metropolitan demand, Shetland knitting has always been expansive, innovatory, connected to the world beyond its island shores. This strong identity, combined with an international outward-looking aspect, has been equally characteristic of Jamieson & Smith's association with hand-knitting, and is clearly illustrated in the present volume. With an eye to both the heritage and the future of the craft, Sarah Laurenson has curated a superb collection, bringing together local luminaries with some of the most familiar names in contemporary knitting. Whether they hail from Brooklyn, Osaka, or from Burra, what all of these contributors share is an appreciation of real Shetland yarn, and the unique design traditions of the Shetland Islands.

The pieces in this volume reveal the wide knitterly potential of Real Shetland Wool. Jean Moss's cables and Jared Flood's twisted stitches are a showcase of Aran texture, while other contributors have chosen to play with the myriad shades of 2 Ply Jumper Weight. Gudrun Johnston's and Mary Jane Mucklestone's designs are warmed with a soft, autumnal palette, while shimmering jewel-tones dance right out of Lesley Smith's wonderful 'Wool Brokers Socks'. Other designers speak directly to different aspects of Shetland's cultural landscape. Sandra Manson's tunic recalls the Isles' Nordic connections: jolly tea pots (surely a quintessential Shetland motif?) wind their way around Masami Yokoyama's cosy, while many-hued waves break across Toshiyuki Shimada and Grace Williamson's fabulous cardigan. And, perhaps most inspiring of all, Lerwick designer, Mary Kay, marks a lifetime's expertise of Shetland wool, and a forty-year association with Jamieson & Smith, with one of her beautiful signature pieces in fine Shetland lace.

Jamieson & Smith have come a long way since Eva set off to buy wool 65 years ago. They ensure that hand-knitting continues to figure centrally in the local culture and economy, spearheading inspiring collaborations, such as the Shetland Fine Lace Project. The company now purchase over 80% of the Isles' annual clip, and, in association with Curtis Wool Direct, are committed to retaining the fibre's sustainable credentials at every processing stage. While the finest grades of wool might end up as Shetland Supreme 1 Ply Laceweight, the coarser grades are put to use in mats and carpeting. Little is wasted, and it all goes back into Shetland's economy, supporting crofting and crofters, and securing a continuing, sustainable future for the sheep on the hills.

Some things happily don't change at Jamieson & Smith. Hand sorting remains as important as it was in Auld Sheepie's day, but the company continues to take new directions by supporting contemporary British design, encouraging local textile talent, and adapting to the interests and expectations of a new generation of knitters worldwide. From its early beginnings at Berry Farm, Jamieson & Smith has always been committed to Real Shetland Wool at every stage from sheep to sweater. This volume is a celebration of that commitment.

—*Kate Davies*

Above: Native Shetland Sheep in the landscape, by well known local photographer, J. D. Rattar (1876 – 1957). Photo courtesy of Shetland Museum and Archives.

Below: Wool waiting to be graded and sorted in the Jamieson & Smith Wool Store. Photo by Jared Flood, 2010.

Wave Cardigan
designed by Toshiyuki Shimada & Grace Williamson

Materials

Jamieson & Smith 2 Ply Jumper Weight – 100% Real Shetland Wool (118m/25g balls)

- Yarn A – Shade 80: 2 (2, 2, 2, 3, 3) x 25g balls
- Yarn B – Shade 4: 2 (2, 2, 2, 2, 2) x 25g balls
- Yarn C – Shade FC58: 2 (2, 2, 2, 2, 2) x 25g balls

All following shades require just 1 x 25g ball in all sizes:

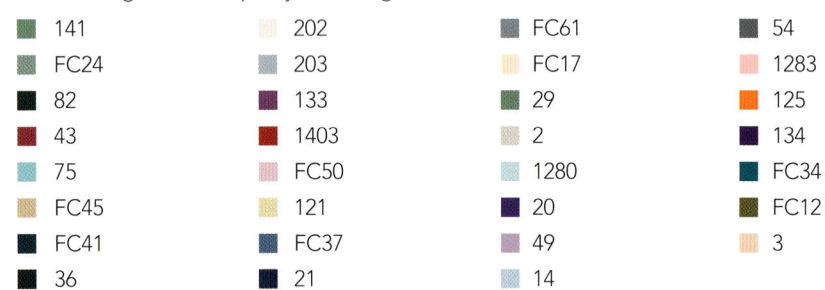

141	202	FC61	54
FC24	203	FC17	1283
82	133	29	125
43	1403	2	134
75	FC50	1280	FC34
FC45	121	20	FC12
FC41	FC37	49	3
36	21	14	

3mm (UK 11/US 2–3) needles (circular or long DPNs)
3.5mm (UK 10–9/US 4) needles (circular or long DPNs)

Stitch markers
Waste yarn or stitch holders
8 (9, 9, 10, 10, 12) buttons
Tapestry needle
Sharp scissors

Abbreviations

See page 76.

Sizing

	XS	S	M	L	1X	2X
Actual bust/chest (cm)	88.5	96	103.5	111	118	125.5
(in)	35	38	41	43.5	46.5	50
Length to underarm (cm)	35	37	37	39	39	41
(in)	14	14.5	14.5	15.5	15.5	16
Finished length (cm)	55	58	59	62.5	63.5	67
(in)	21.5	23	23.25	24.5	25	26.5
Sleeve* (cm)	43	43	43	43	43	43
(in)	17	17	17	17	17	17

Size shown in photographs is L (111cm/43.5in bust/chest).
*Sleeve is measured from shoulder.

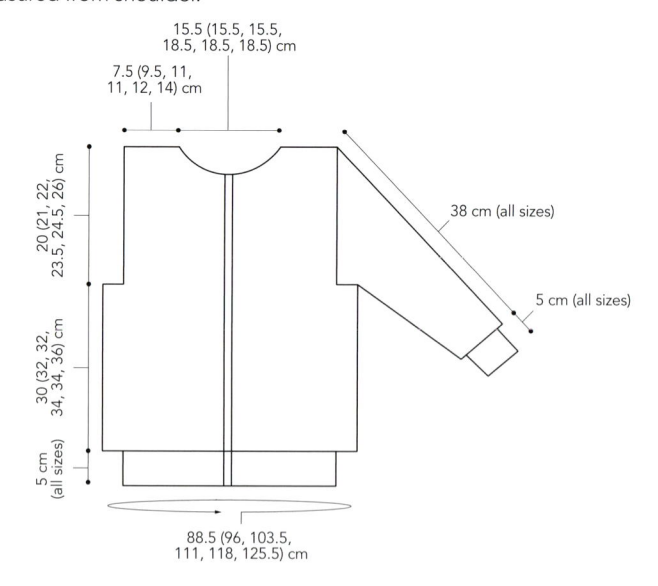

Tension

32.5 sts and 32.5 rows = 10cm/4in over Fair Isle pattern using 3.5mm needles.

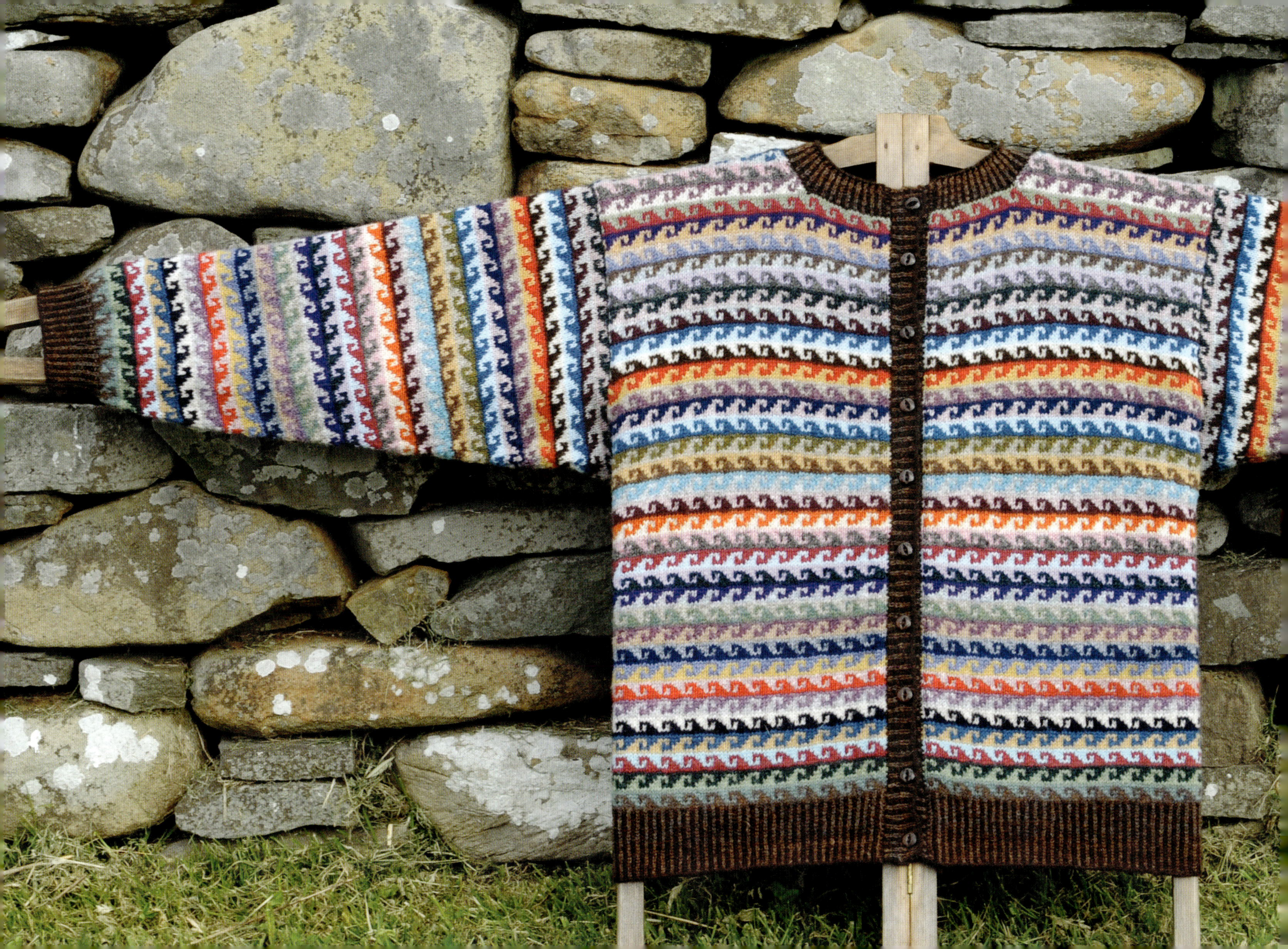

Body Colour Guide

Round numbers	Colour 1	Colour 2	Colour 3	Colour 4
1–10	FC58	141	FC24	82
11–20	43	75	FC45	FC41
21–30	36	202	203	133
31–40	1403	FC50	121	FC37
41–50	21	FC61	FC17	133
51–60	29	2	1280	20
61–70	82	49	14	43
71–80	54	1283	202	125
81–90	134	FC50	1280	FC34
91–100	4	FC45	2	FC12
101–110	FC41	14	FC50	21
111–120	133	2	121	1403
121–130	80	202	14	FC41
131–140	134	1280	1283	82
141–150	54	49	1280	FC58
151–160	FC37	3	FC45	20
161–170	43	FC24	202	133
171–180	54	1283	1280	FC41
181–190	36	3	FC58	141
191–200	FC24	82	43	75
201–210	FC45	FC41	36	202

Sleeve Colour Guide

Round numbers	Colour 1	Colour 2	Colour 3	Colour 4
1–10	80	202	121	1403
11–20	133	2	FC50	21
21–30	FC41	14	2	FC12
31–40	4	FC45	1280	FC34
41–50	134	FC50	202	125
51–60	54	1283	14	43
61–70	82	49	1280	20
71–80	29	2	FC17	133
81–90	21	FC61	121	FC37
91–100	1403	FC50	203	133
101–110	36	202	FC45	FC41
111–120	43	75	FC24	82
121–125	FC58	141		

Chart Key

- ■ Colour 1
- ☐ Colour 2
- ● Colour 3
- ☒ Colour 4
- ▢ Pattern repeat

Chart A

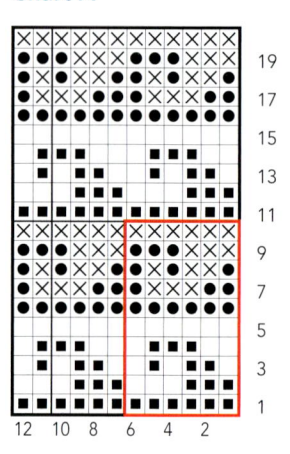

To knit Wave Cardigan

Body

Using yarn A and 3mm needles, cast on 263 (283, 305, 331, 347, 367) sts (includes 10 steek sts). Join to work in the round, taking care not to twist sts. Place marker for start of round, the first 5 sts and last 5 sts of the round are the steek sts.

Rnd 1: (K1A, K1B) twice, K1A, pm, *K1B, P1A; rep from * to last 6 sts, K1B, pm, (K1A, K1B) twice, K1A.

Last round sets steek stitches (10 sts between markers just placed) and corrugated rib with yarns A and B. Work 8 more rounds as set.

Rnd 10: (K1A, K1C) twice, K1A, slm, *K1C, P1A; rep from * to last 6 sts, K1C, slm, (K1A, K1C) twice, K1A.

Work 10 more rounds as set using yarns A and C.

Change to 3.5mm needles.

Rnd 21: Using yarn C only, K5, slm, *K7 (7, 7, 8, 7, 7), M1; rep from * to last 8 (0, 8, 9, 8, 0) sts before marker, K8 (0, 8, 9, 8, 0), slm, K5. 298 (322, 346, 370, 394, 418) sts (including 10 steek sts).

From this point onwards, the steek sts should be worked in alternating knit stitches using shades as set by the colourwork pattern. Change colours at start of round. There is no need to weave in ends as they will simply be trimmed later.

Rnd 1: Work 5 steek sts, slm, using shades as indicated in the Body Colour Guide, work in pattern from row 1 of chart A, repeating the marked 6-stitch Fair Isle motif 48 (52, 56, 60, 64, 68) times, slm, work 5 steek sts.

Last round sets steek pattern and chart A motif. Continue to work from chart A, using colours as indicated in the Body Colour Guide, until 98 (104, 104, 110, 110, 116) rounds in Fair Isle pattern have been worked in total.

Shape armholes

Next rnd: Using shades as indicated in the Body Colour Guide, work 5 steek sts, slm, work 65 (71, 75, 81, 85, 91) sts in colourwork pattern from chart as set, pm, slip next 14 (14, 18, 18, 22, 22) sts to waste yarn for underarm and cast on 10 steek sts using alternating colours, pm, work 130 (142, 150, 162, 170, 182) sts in colourwork pattern as set, pm, slip next 14 (14, 18, 18, 22, 22) sts to waste yarn for underarm and cast on 10 steek sts using alternating colours, pm, work last 65 (71, 75, 81, 85, 91) sts in colourwork pattern, slm, work 5 steek sts as set. 290 (314, 330, 354, 370, 394) sts (including 30 steek sts).

Next rnd: Work 5 steek sts, slm, *work in colourwork patt as set to marker, slm, work 10 steek sts in alternating colours, slm; rep from * once more, work in colourwork patt as set to marker, slm, work 5 steek sts.

Next rnd: Work 5 steek sts, slm, *work in colourwork patt as set to 2 sts before marker, K2tog, slm, work 10 steek sts, slm, SSK; rep from * once more, work in colourwork patt as set to marker, slm, work 5 steek sts. 286 (310, 326, 350, 366, 390) sts (including 30 steek sts).

Repeat last 2 rounds 4 more times, using colours as indicated in the Body Colour Guide. 270 (294, 310, 334, 350, 374) sts (including 30 steek sts).

Then work 32 (35, 38, 43, 46, 51) more rounds in pattern without shaping.

Shape neck

Next rnd: Work as set to 5 sts before end of round, slm, cast off final 5 steek sts, as well as first 5 steek sts of start of next round.

Next rnd: Slip first 20 (20, 20, 25, 25, 25) sts of round to waste yarn for front neck. Using new shades, cast on 10 steek sts, pm, continue to work colourwork patt as set to armhole steek marker, slm, work 10 steek sts, slm, work in colourwork patt as set to marker, slm, work 10 steek sts, slm, work in colourwork patt to last 20 (20, 20, 25, 25, 25) sts before marker and slip these last 20 (20, 20, 25, 25, 25) sts to waste yarn for front neck. 230 (254, 270, 284, 300, 324) sts (including 30 steek sts).

Work as previously set, decreasing 1 st at each side of front neck steek on 5 following alternate rounds. 220 (244, 260, 274, 290, 314) sts (including 30 steek sts).

Next rnd: Work as set to end of first armhole steek, slm, work in colourwork patt over 35 (41, 45, 46, 50, 56) sts, slip next 50 (50, 50, 60, 60, 60) sts to waste yarn for back neck, pm, cast on 10 steek sts using alternate colours, pm, work in patt as set to end of round. 180 (204, 220, 224, 240, 264) sts (including 40 steek sts).

Dec 1 st at each side of both front and back neck steeks on next 10 rounds. Cast off each set of 10 steek sts on final round. You will have 4 sets of 25 (31, 35, 36, 40, 46) shoulder sts remaining.

Graft left front and back shoulders together using Kitchener stitch, then repeat for right front and back shoulders.

Cutting the steeks

Using sharp scissors, cut each steek between the 5th and 6th stitches. Neatly trim ends left from changing colours. Turn to WS and carefully sew down each side of the steek.

Sleeves

Work both sleeves alike.

Please note: The colour sequence for sleeves is worked in reverse from the body sequence. If you require longer (or shorter) sleeves, you will need to adjust where you begin the sequence so that it ends on the same row.

Using 3.5mm needles and shade 80 and starting in the centre of the stitches on waste yarn for the armhole, K7 (7, 9, 9, 11, 11) from waste yarn, pick up and knit 59 (62, 63, 69, 73, 76) sts evenly up to shoulder, then pick up and knit 59 (62, 63, 69, 73, 76) sts back down to underarm, K7 (7, 9, 9, 11, 11) from waste yarn. 132 (138, 144, 156, 168, 174) sts.

Rnd 1: Using colours as specified in the Sleeve Colour Guide, work from chart, repeating the 6-stitch motif 22 (23, 24, 26, 28, 29) times in each round.

Work 6 more rounds in pattern as set.

Rnd 8: SSK, work in patt as set to last 2 sts, K2tog. 130 (136, 142, 154, 166, 172) sts.

Dec 1 st at each end of 29 following 4th rounds as set, using shades as specified in the Sleeve Colour Guide. 72 (78, 84, 96, 108, 114) sts.

Rnd 125 (dec): Using yarn C only, *K1, K2tog; rep from * to end of round. 48 (52, 56, 64, 72, 76) sts.

Change to 3mm needles.

Rnd 1: *K1C, P1A; rep from * to end.

Repeat this round 6 more times.

Rnd 8: *K1B, P1A; rep from * to end.

Repeat this round 8 more times.

Cast off in rib using yarn A only.

Neckband

With RS facing, using 3mm needles and yarn C, K20 (20, 20, 25, 25, 25) sts from right front neck waste yarn, pick up and knit 30 sts from neck edge, K50 (50, 50, 60, 60, 60) sts from back neck waste yarn, pick up and knit 30 sts from neck edge, K20 (20, 20, 25, 25, 25) sts from left front waste yarn. 150 (150, 150, 170, 170, 170) sts.

Row 1 (WS): P10 (10, 10, 4, 4, 4), *P2tog, P2 (2, 2, 3, 3, 3); rep from * 32 more times, P8 (8, 8, 1, 1, 1). 117 (117, 117, 137, 137, 137) sts.

Row 2 (RS): *K1C, P1A; rep from * to last st, K1C.

Row 3: *P1C, K1A; rep from * to last st, P1C.

Repeat last 2 rows once more.

Row 6: *K1B, P1A; rep from * to last st, K1B.

Row 7: *P1B, K1A; rep from * to last st, P1B.

Repeat last 2 rows twice more.

Cast off in rib using yarn A only.

Button band

With RS facing, starting at edge of neckband, using 3mm needles and yarn C, pick up and knit 120 (128, 130, 138, 140, 148) sts evenly down front edge to cast-on edge.

Row 1 (WS): Purl.

Row 2 (RS): *K1C, P1A; rep from * to end.

Row 3: *K1A, P1C; rep from * to end.

Repeat last 2 rows once more.

Row 6: *K1B, P1A; rep from * to end.

Row 7: *K1A, P1B; rep from * to end.

Repeat last 2 rows twice more.

Cast off in rib using yarn A only.

Buttonhole band

With RS facing, starting at cast-on edge, using 3mm needles and yarn C, pick up and knit 120 (128, 130, 138, 140, 148) sts evenly up front edge to neckband.

Work rows 1–4 as for button band.

Row 5 (WS): Rib as set over 3 (3, 4, 5, 6, 1) sts, cast off 2 sts, *rib as set over 14 (13, 13, 12, 12, 11) sts (including st remaining from previous cast off), cast off 2 sts; rep from * 6 (7, 7, 8, 8, 10) more times, rib to end.

Row 6: Using yarns B and A, work in rib as set, casting on 2 sts over each of those cast off on previous row.

Work 5 more rows in rib as for button band.

Cast off in rib using yarn A only.

Finishing

Darn in any remaining ends. Sew buttons to button band to match buttonholes. Wash (see page 79).

If desired, block cardigan over a woolly board.

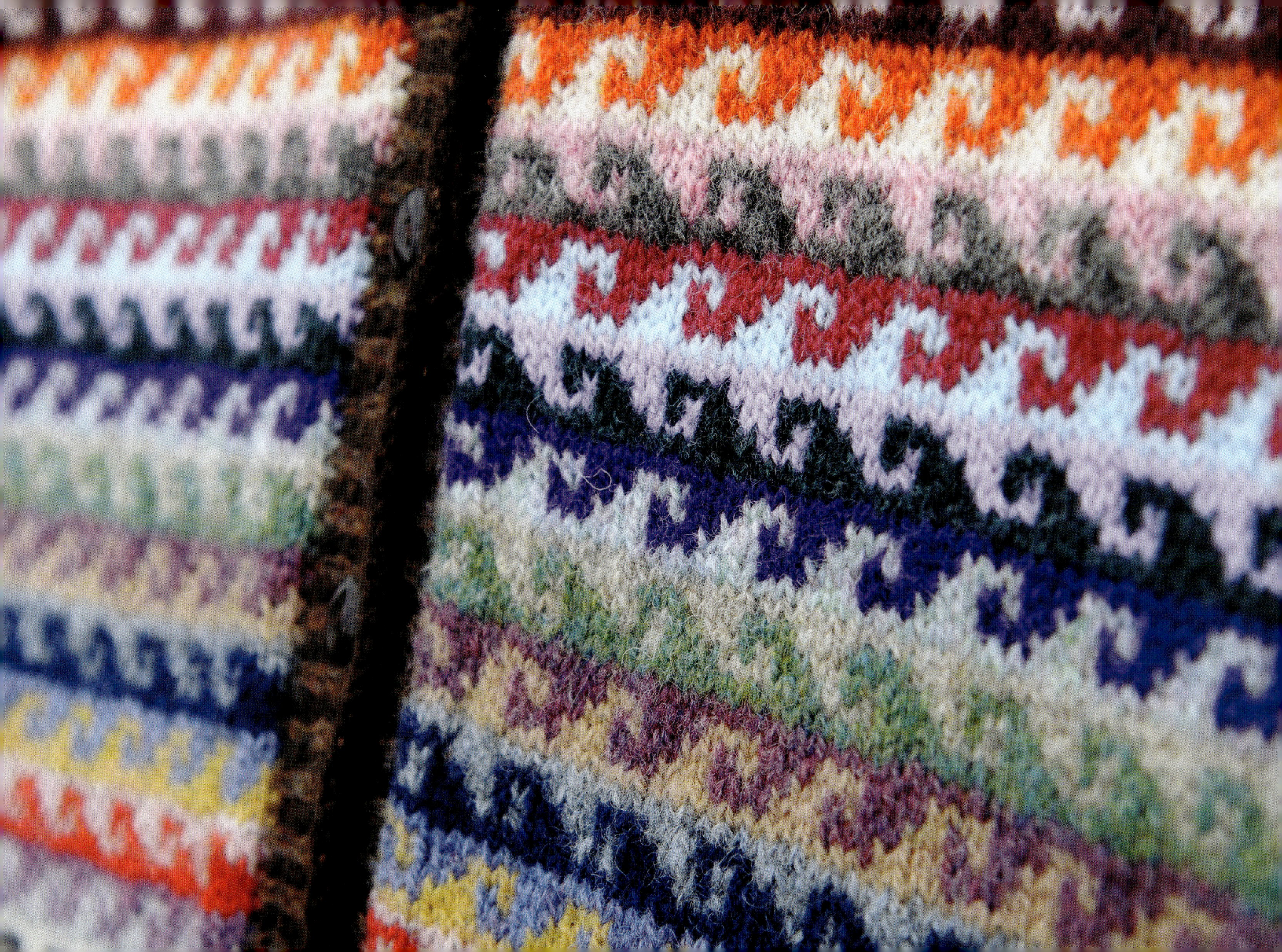

Feathercrest Mittens
designed by Jared Flood

Materials

Jamieson & Smith Shetland Aran – 100% Real Shetland Wool (90m/50g balls)

- Shade BSS1: 2 x 50g balls

5mm (UK 6/US 8) DPNs (or your preferred needles for small diameter working in the round)
Cable needle
Tapestry needle
Length of waste yarn

Sizing

One size only

Hand circumference: 19.5cm/7.75in

Length from cuff to fingertips: 24cm/9.5in

Tension

18 sts & 26 rows = 10cm/4in over reverse st st in the round, using 5mm needles

Abbreviations

See page 76.

To knit Feathercrest Mittens

Right mitten

Using 5mm needles cast on 34 sts. Join to work in the round, taking care not to twist sts. Place marker for start of round.

Rnd 1: *P1, K1 tbl; rep from * to end of round.

Last round sets 1x1 twisted rib. Work in 1x1 twisted rib until piece meas 5cm/2in from cast-on edge.

Work round 1 of chart A (right mitten), increasing 4 sts as indicated. 38 sts.

Now work rounds 2–20 of chart A.

On round 21 of chart, you will use a short length of waste yarn to hold stitches for thumb.

Rnd 21: Work 21 sts in pattern, thus reaching the sts indicated on the chart. Using waste yarn K7, now slip these 7 sts that have just been worked back to left-hand needle. Using main yarn, purl these 7 sts again. Now continue in pattern as directed by chart to the end of round.

You will now have 7 sts of waste yarn in your fabric. After the completion of chart A, you will come back to these stitches, unpick the waste yarn, and work an 'afterthought' thumb.

Work rounds 22–51 of chart A. 18 sts.

Turn mitten inside out and place first 9 sts on one needle. With the remaining 9 sts on a second needle, use a third needle to knit together the first stitch from each needle. *Knit together the next stitch from each needle. You will now have 2 sts on right-hand needle, cast off 1 st in the normal way. Rep from * until all of the mitten stitches have been cast off. Break yarn and fasten off.

Right thumb

Carefully unpick the 7-stitch section of waste yarn at thumb, placing stitches from row below on one needle, and stitches from row above on another. Pick up an extra stitch at the left-hand end of the lower needle. 15 sts.

Distribute the sts evenly over your needles.

Starting on right-hand side of thumb opening (with palm of glove facing and cuff pointing down), join in working yarn and work rounds 1–8 of chart B (right thumb). 14 sts.

Purl 6 rounds (add more rounds here for a longer thumb).

Next rnd: P2, (P2tog, P1) 4 times. 10 sts.

Next rnd: (P2tog) 5 times. 5 sts.

Break yarn leaving a 12.5cm/5in tail. Using a tapestry needle, thread yarn tail through 5 live sts and pull tightly to snugly close thumb.

Left mitten

Using 5mm needles cast on 34 sts. Join to work in the round, taking care not to twist sts. Place marker for start of round.

Rnd 1: *K1 tbl, P1; rep from * to end of round.

Last round sets 1x1 twisted rib. Work in 1x1 twisted rib until piece meas 5cm/2in from cast-on edge.

Work round 1 of chart C (left mitten), increasing 4 sts as indicated. 38 sts.

Now work rounds 2–20 of chart C.

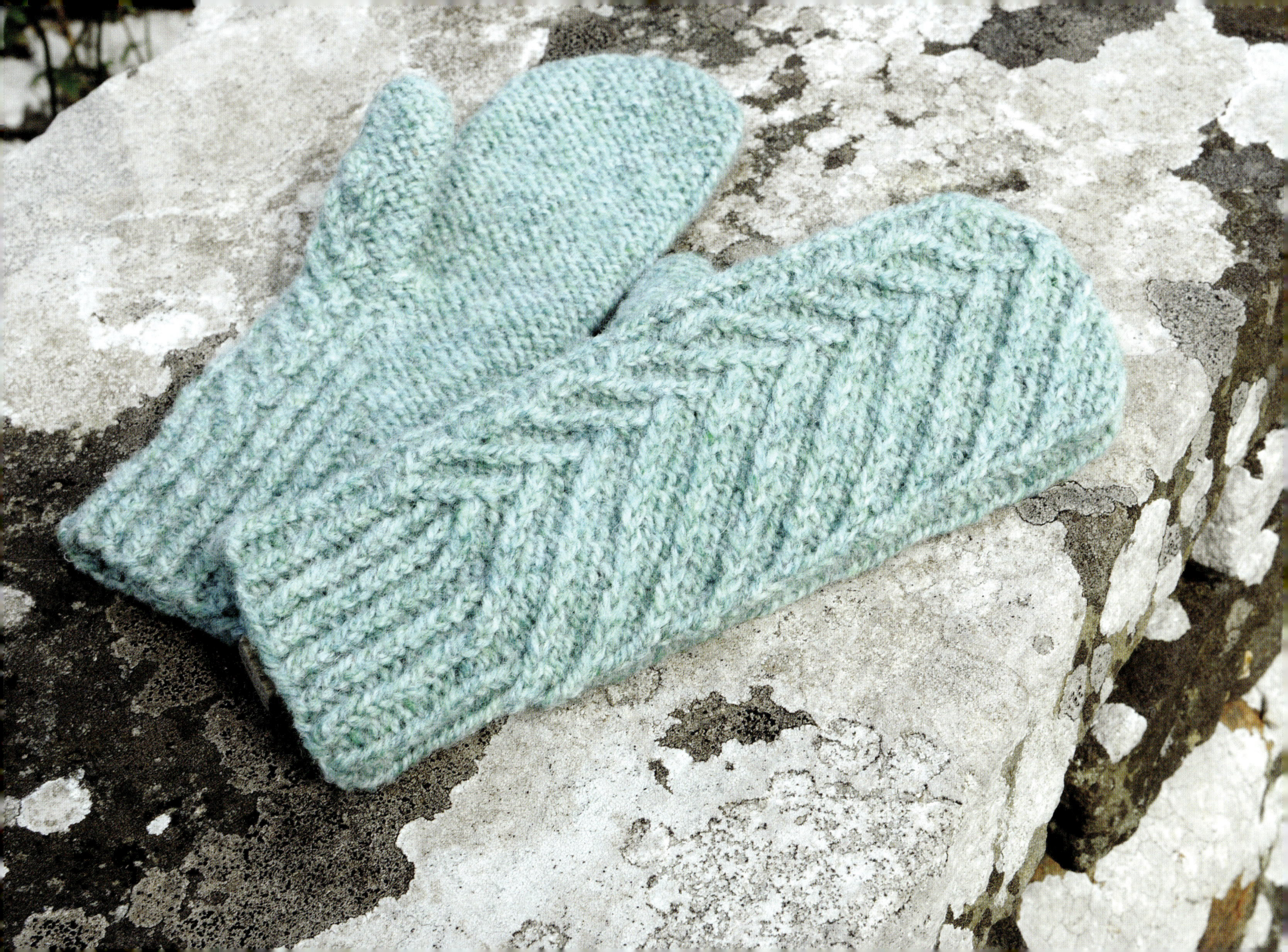

On round 21 of chart, you will use a short length of waste yarn to hold stitches for thumb.

Rnd 21: Work 10 sts in pattern, thus reaching the sts indicated on the chart. Using waste yarn K7, now slip these 7 sts that have just been worked back to left-hand needle. Using main yarn, purl these 7 sts again. Now continue in pattern as directed by chart to the end of round.

You will now have 7 sts of waste yarn in your fabric. After the completion of chart C, you will come back to these stitches, unpick the waste yarn, and work an 'afterthought' thumb.

Work rounds 22–51 of chart C. 18 sts.

Turn mitten inside out and place first 9 sts on one needle. With the remaining 9 sts on a second needle, use a third needle to knit together the first stitch from each needle. *Knit together the next stitch from each needle. You will now have 2 sts on right-hand needle, cast off 1 st in the normal way. Rep from * until all of the mitten stitches have been cast off. Break yarn and fasten off.

Left thumb

Carefully unpick the 7-stitch section of waste yarn at thumb, placing stitches from row below on one needle, and stitches from row above on another. Pick up an extra stitch at the left-hand end of the lower needle. 15 sts.

Distribute the sts evenly over your needles.

Starting on right-hand side of thumb opening (with palm of glove facing and cuff pointing down), join in working yarn and work rounds 1–8 of chart D (left thumb). 14 sts.

Purl 6 rounds (add more rounds here for a longer thumb).

Next rnd: P2tog, P3, (P2tog, P1) 3 times. 10 sts.

Next rnd: (P2tog) 5 times. 5 sts.

Break yarn leaving a 12.5cm/5in tail. Using a tapestry needle, thread yarn tail through 5 live sts and pull tightly to snugly close thumb.

Finishing

Darn any holes at the base of the thumbs and darn in all ends.

Chart Key

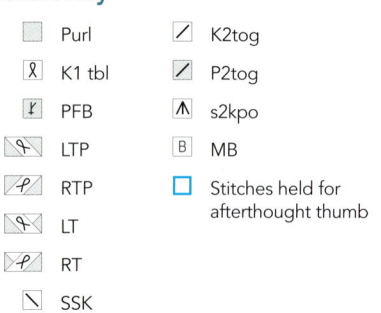

- Purl
- K1 tbl
- PFB
- LTP
- RTP
- LT
- RT
- SSK
- K2tog
- P2tog
- s2kpo
- MB
- Stitches held for afterthought thumb

Chart A (Right Mitten)

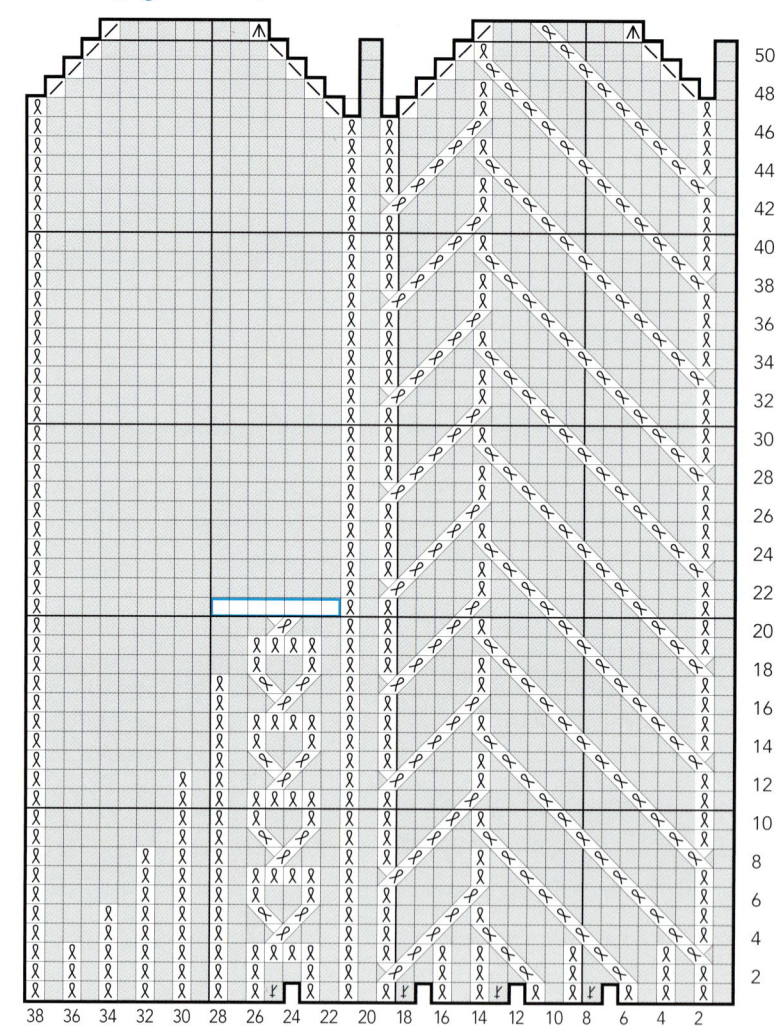

Chart B (Right Thumb)

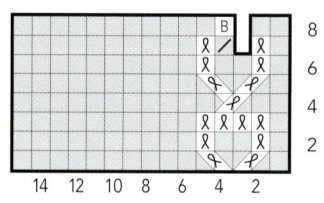

Chart C (Left Mitten)

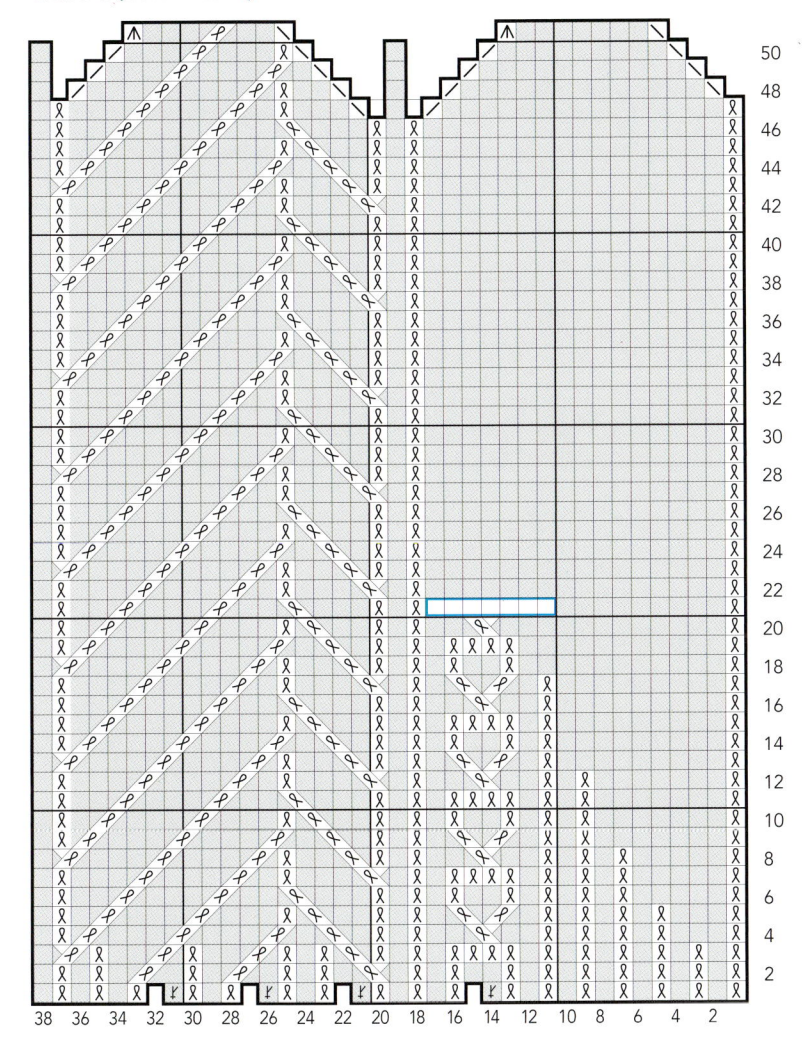

Chart D (Left Thumb)

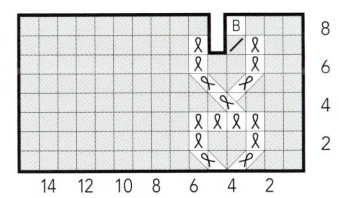

Peat Hill Waistcoat
designed by Hazel Tindall

Materials

Jamieson & Smith Shetland Supreme 2 Ply Jumper Weight – 100% Real Shetland Wool (172m/50g balls)

- Yarn A – Shade 2005: 2 x 50g balls
- Yarn B – Shade 2003: 1 x 50g ball
- Yarn C – Shade 2001: 1 x 50g ball
- Yarn D – Shade 2004: 1 x 50g ball
- Yarn E – Shade 2006: 1 x 50g ball
- Yarn F – Shade 2009: 1 x 50g ball

2.75mm (UK 12/US 2) circular needle, 80cm/32in long

3.5mm (UK 10–9/US 4) DPNs or circular needle, 60cm/24in long

4mm (UK 8/US G/6) crochet hook

Stitch holders
Stitch markers
Tapestry needle
A length of cotton
Sharp scissors

Sizing

One size only

Actual bust (cm)	97.5
(in)	38.5
Actual length (cm)	52.5
(in)	21

Tension

30 sts & 31 rows = 10cm/4in over Fair Isle pattern using 3.5mm needles

Abbreviations

See page 76.

Pattern notes

Waistcoat can be worn open or overlapping and fastened with a brooch. As a result it will fit bust sizes from 81cm/32in to 102cm/40in.

This pattern uses a provisional crochet cast on, which is worked as foll:

Using 4mm crochet hook and smooth cotton, chain 222 sts, cut the cotton and pull through the last loop. Using yarn A and 3.25mm circular needle, pick up and knit 219 sts into the loops at the back of the chain.

If you wish, you can use a conventional cast-on method instead.

When changing yarns, it is best to change the colours between the 4th and 5th steek stitches, as these can be trimmed later with no need for weaving in.

To knit Peat Hill Waistcoat

Body

Work a provisional crochet cast on as described above, or using 3.5mm needles and yarn A, cast on 219 sts. Place a marker. Using the backwards loop method, cast on 9 steek stitches, and place another marker. 228 sts (including 9 steek sts).

Join to work in the round, taking care not to twist sts. Join in yarn B, leaving a 10cm/4in tail.

Rnd 1: Work chart row 1 from right to left, repeat the marked 22-st pattern repeat 9 times in total, then work a further 6 sts in patt (the sts at the end of the round will mirror the those at the start), slm, knit 9 steek sts in alternating colours.

Rnd 2: K1 in yarn A, M1, then work chart row 2 from right to left, in pattern as set to last st before marker, M1, K1 in yarn A, slm, knit 9 steek sts in alternating colours. 230 sts (including 9 steek sts).

Rnds 3 – 27: Work colour pattern and increases as set by last round. 280 sts (including 9 steek sts).

Rnd 28: Work chart row 28 to marker, slm, knit 9 steek sts in alternating colours.

Rnd 29: K1 in yarn A, M1, work chart row 29 to last st before marker, M1, K1 in yarn A, slm, knit 9 steek sts in alternating colours. 282 sts (including 9 steek sts)

Last 2 rounds set increases on alternate rounds. Work 10 more increases on alternate rounds as set (20 more rounds worked). 302 sts (including 9 steek sts).

Rnds 50 – 85: Continue to work from chart, with no further shaping.

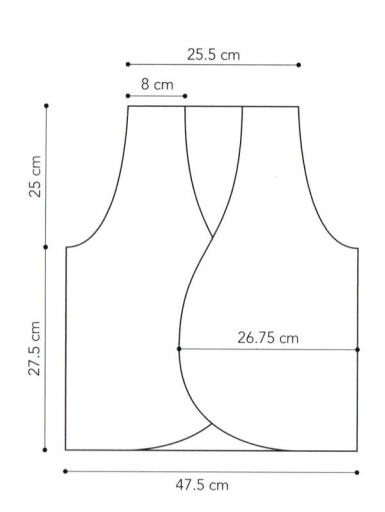

Measurements DO NOT include trim, which is 1.5 cm on all edges.

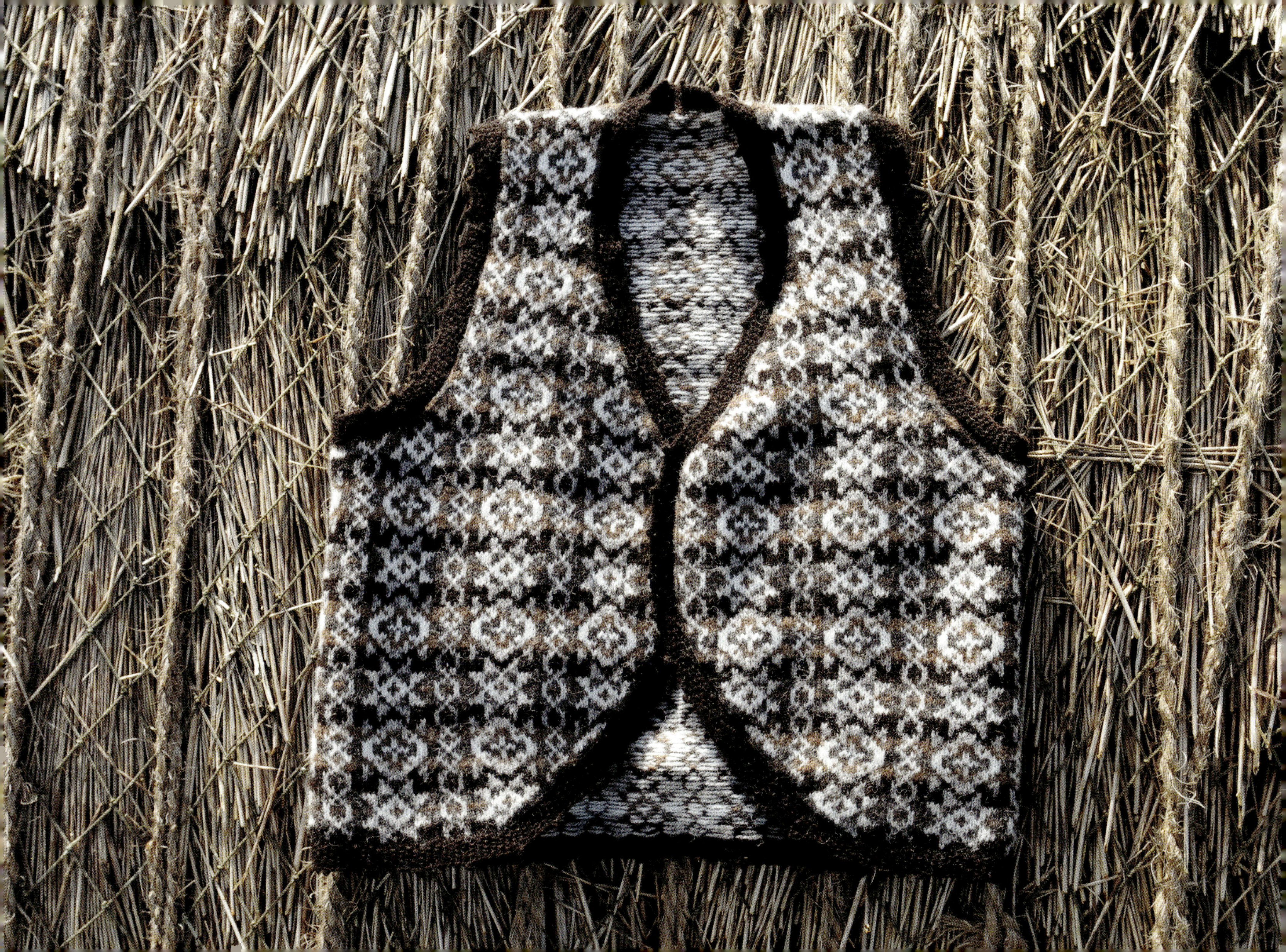

Shape armholes

Rnd 86: Following chart row 86, work 67 sts in pattern, pm, slip next 27 sts to a holder, using the backwards loop method, cast on 9 steek sts, pm, keeping pattern correct, work 105 back sts in patt, pm, slip next 27 sts to holder, using backwards loop method, cast on 9 steek sts, pm, keeping pattern correct work to marker, slm, work 9 steek sts in alternating colours. 266 sts (including 27 steek sts).

Dec 1 st at all 4 armhole edges on next 14 rounds, and **at the same time** dec 1 st at front edges on 3rd round and 10 foll rounds, then on 18 following alt rounds. 152 sts (including 27 steek sts).

You should now have 24 sts remaining on the fronts, and 77 sts remaining on the back (plus 27 steek sts).

Work 27 rounds without further shaping, and at the end of the last round, cast off the final 5 steek sts.

Rnd 163: Work pattern to armhole marker, cast off 9 steek sts, knit across the back to armhole marker, cast off 9 steek sts, knit to centre front, cast off remaining steek sts, break yarn and pull both colours through the last st.

Using sharp scissors, cut the centre front steek through the centre of the middle stitch. Trim ends neatly. Turn to WS and neatly sew down each side of the steek.

Place centre 29 sts of back onto waste yarn whilst joining the shoulder seams using yarn D. The seams can be joined either using the three-needle cast-off method, or by grafting the sts using Kitchener stitch.

Border

Using 2.75mm needle and yarn A, start at the bottom of the right front and working up the front edge, pick up and knit 163 sts to shoulder seam (one st for every row knitted), knit across the 29 back neck sts, pick up and knit one 163 sts down left front to cast-on edge, (1 st for every row), pm, unravel the provisional cast-on edge and pick up and knit the 219 sts revealed as you go (or pick up and knit 1 st in every cast-on st if a conventional cast-on method was used). 574 sts.

Join to work in the round, and place marker for start of round.

Rnd 1: K7, (K2tog, K2) 39 times, K2tog, K25, K2tog, (K2, K2tog) 39 times, K7, slm, K5, (K2tog, K2) 52 times, K2tog, K4. 441 sts.

**Rnd 2: *K1, P1; rep from * to last st, K1.

Rnd 3: *P1, K1; rep from * to last st, P1.

These 2 rounds set moss st (US seed st). Work a further 6 rounds in moss st.

Cast off as foll:

Change to 3.5mm needles. Cast off 5 sts, *(insert point of left needle into the st on the right needle, yo right needle, slip the stitch over the yo and off the needle, leaving one st on the right needle) twice, then insert point of right needle into the base st to give two sts on the right needle, and pass the furthest right st over the left, cast off 6; rep from * until the marker and check that casting off 6 between each picot will work evenly. If not, just cast off fewer sts to make the spaces between picots even.**

Armhole borders

Using sharp scissors, cut armhole steek through the centre of the middle st. Trim ends neatly. Turn to WS and neatly sew down each side of the steek.

With RS facing, start at the side slope left of the st holder. Using 2.75mm circular needle and yarn A, pick up and knit 78 sts to shoulder seam, pick up and knit 78 sts down to underarm, pm, knit the 27 stitches from the holder. 183 sts.

Join to work in the round and place marker for start of round.

Rnd 1: (K2tog, K2) 39 times, K2tog, K25. 143 sts.

Now work as for main border from ** to **.

Finishing

Darn in any remaining ends. Using cotton yarn and tapestry needle put a thread through all picots on both armhole openings and tie in a bow. Thread another length of cotton through picots at neck edge, starting from decreases on the right side, round back of neck and down left side to start of decreases.

Wash (see page 79).

Put two oblong pillows in a plastic bag and cover with a towel (this should be slightly wider than the waistcoat).

Put the waistcoat over the towel covered pillows, gently easing/stretching it to shape. Using stainless steel pins, and starting at the straight edges at the centre front, pin the picots to the pillows. Work downwards, pinning each picot to the pillow until all unthreaded picots are pinned. Keep checking the shape. Open the thread bow at the neck picots and gently pull to get an even shape, re-tie and pin where needed to get a good shape at the centre front. Do the same with each armhole opening. Check that the waistcoat is smooth, and adjust pins as necessary. Allow to dry thoroughly before un-pinning.

Chart Key

- Yarn A (2005); Knit
- Yarn B (2003); Knit
- Yarn C (2001); Knit
- Yarn D (2004); Knit
- Yarn E (2006); Knit
- Yarn F (2009); Knit
- Pattern repeat

Chart A

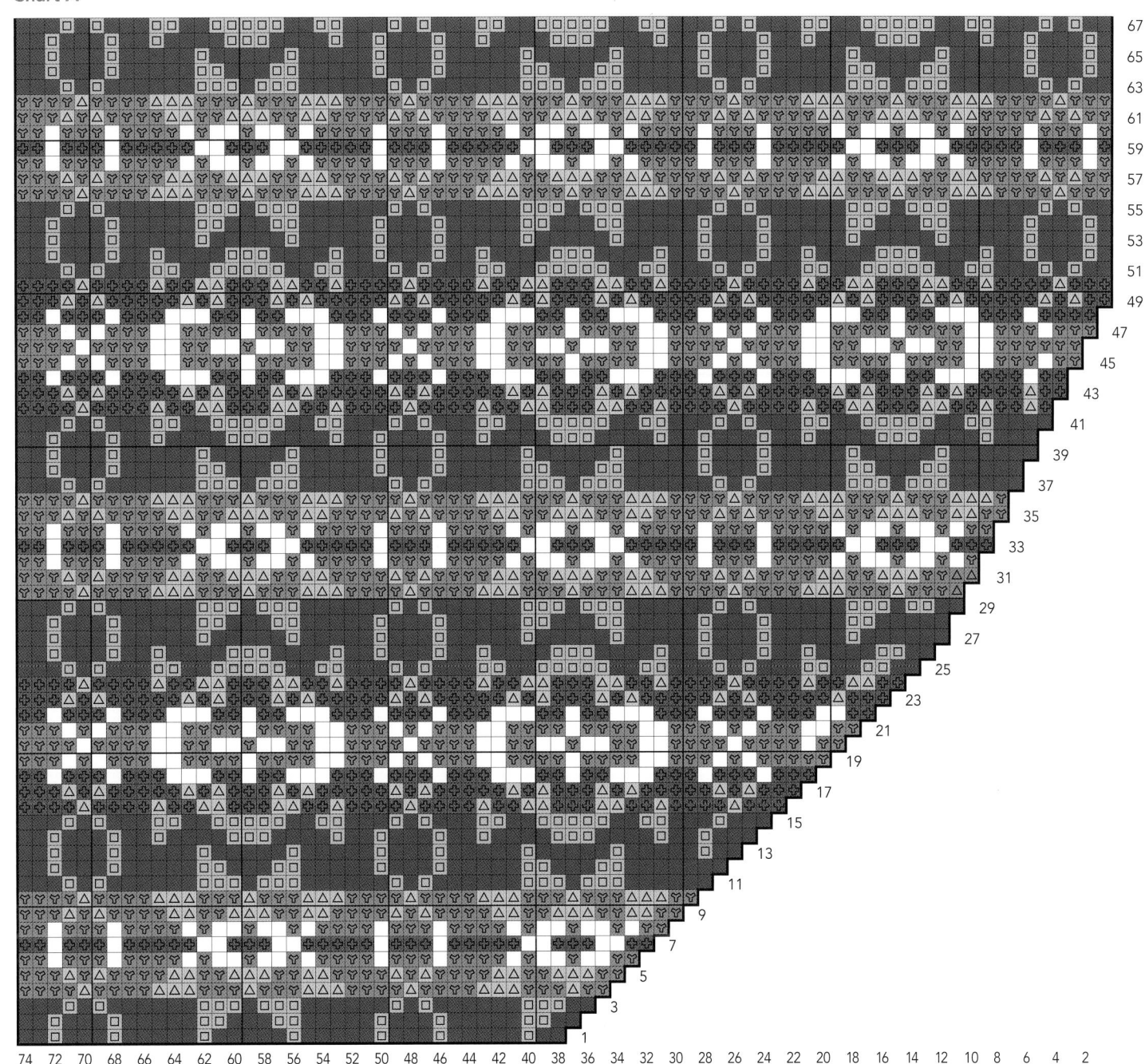

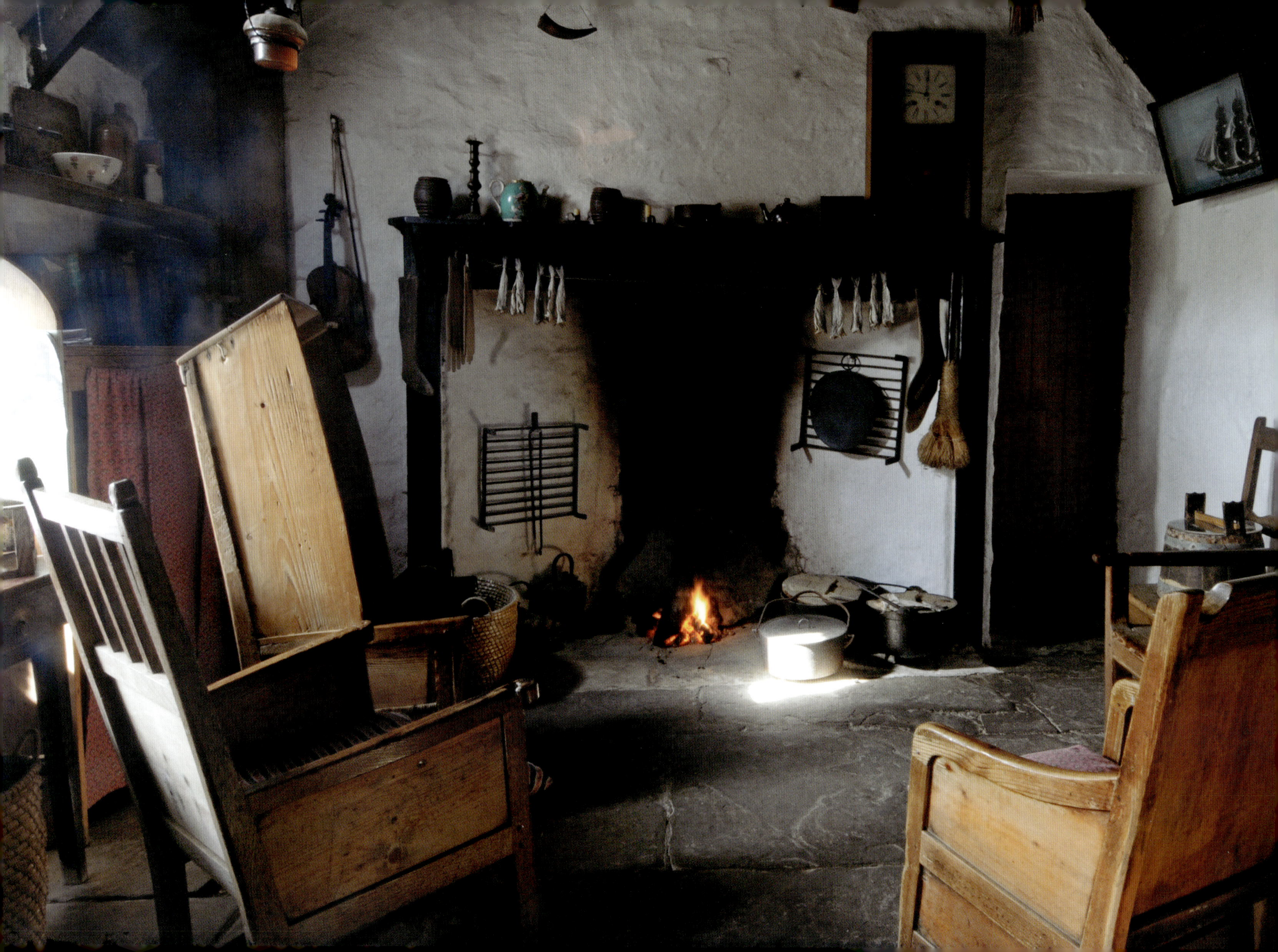

Chart A continued

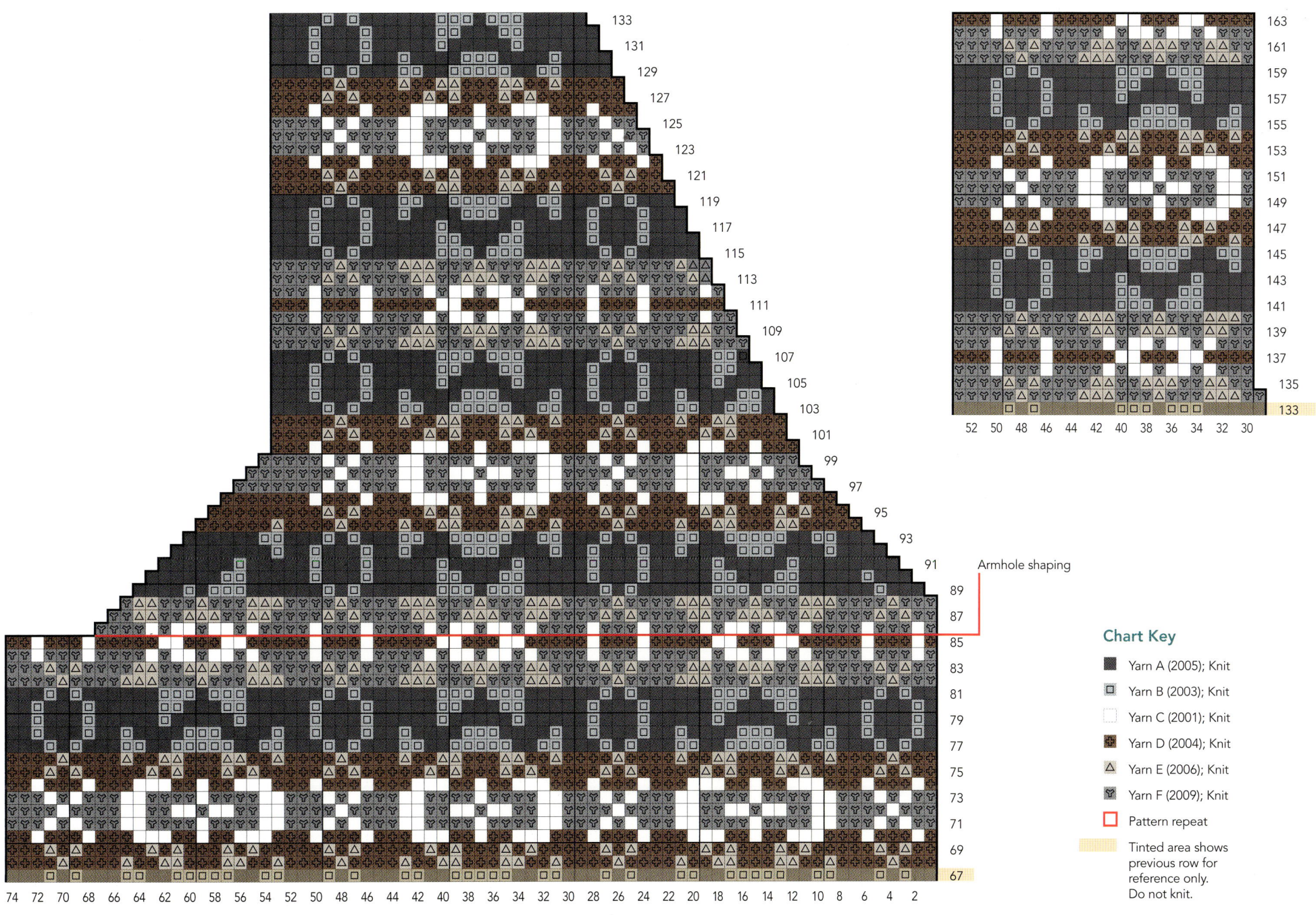

Chart A continued

Chart Key

- ■ Yarn A (2005); Knit
- ▢ Yarn B (2003); Knit
- ☐ Yarn C (2001); Knit
- ✚ Yarn D (2004); Knit
- △ Yarn E (2006); Knit
- ♈ Yarn F (2009); Knit
- ▭ Pattern repeat
- Tinted area shows previous row for reference only. Do not knit.

Armhole shaping

Cross Tam
designed by Daniel Goldman

Materials

Jamieson & Smith 2 Ply Jumper Weight – 100% Real Shetland Wool (118m/25g balls)

- Yarn A – Shade 82: 1 x 25g ball
- Yarn B – Shade 34: 1 x 25g ball
- Yarn C – Shade 29: 1 x 25g ball
- Yarn D – Shade 122: 1 x 25g ball
- Yarn E – Shade FC38: 1 x 25g ball

2.5mm (UK 13–12/US 1–2) DPNs
2.5mm (UK 13–12/US 1–2) circular needle, approx. 20 or 30cm long
2mm (UK 14/US 0) circular needle, approx. 20 or 30cm long

2mm (US B/1) crochet hook

Dinner plate or cardboard disk for blocking

Sizing

One size only

To fit an average adult head circumference: 50–55cm/19.5–20.5in

Actual circumference at brim: 52cm/20.5in

Tension

28 sts and 30 rounds = 10cm/4in over Fair Isle pattern using 2.5mm needles

Abbreviations

See page 76.

To knit Cross Tam

With 2mm crochet hook and yarn D, create 7 stitches using Emily Ocker's circular cast-on method.

Change to 2.5mm DPNs.

Rnd 1: (KFB) 7 times. 14 sts.

Rnd 2: (KFB) 14 times. 28 sts.

Now work chart A as foll:

Rnd 1: Work from row 1 of chart A, repeating the chart 7 times in the round.

Cont to work from chart A as set, working increases as indicated on alternate rounds, until round 45 is complete. 182 sts.

Change to 2.5mm circular needles if it is more comfortable to do so.

Next rnd: Using yarn B *K89, K2tog; rep from * once more. 180 sts.

Next rnd: Work from row 1 of chart B, repeating the motif 45 times in the round.

Cont to work from chart B until row 9 is complete.

Next rnd: Using yarn B only, *K3, K2tog; rep from * to end of round. 144 sts.

Change to 2mm circular needles.

Next rnd: Using yarn A only, *K1, P1; rep from * to end of round.

Last round sets rib. Work 9 more rounds as set.

The Tam is completed with a tubular cast off which is worked as foll:

Rnd 1: *K1, Sl 1 purlwise with yarn in front; rep from * to end.

Rnd 2: *Sl 1 purlwise with yarn in back, P1; rep from * to end.

Repeat these two rounds once more.

Slip all knit sts to one set of needles and all purl sts to another set. Holding the needles parallel, cast off by grafting the knit and purl stitches together using Kitchener stitch.

Finishing

Darn in all ends.

Wash (see page 79) and block over a dinner plate or stiff cardboard disk to dry.

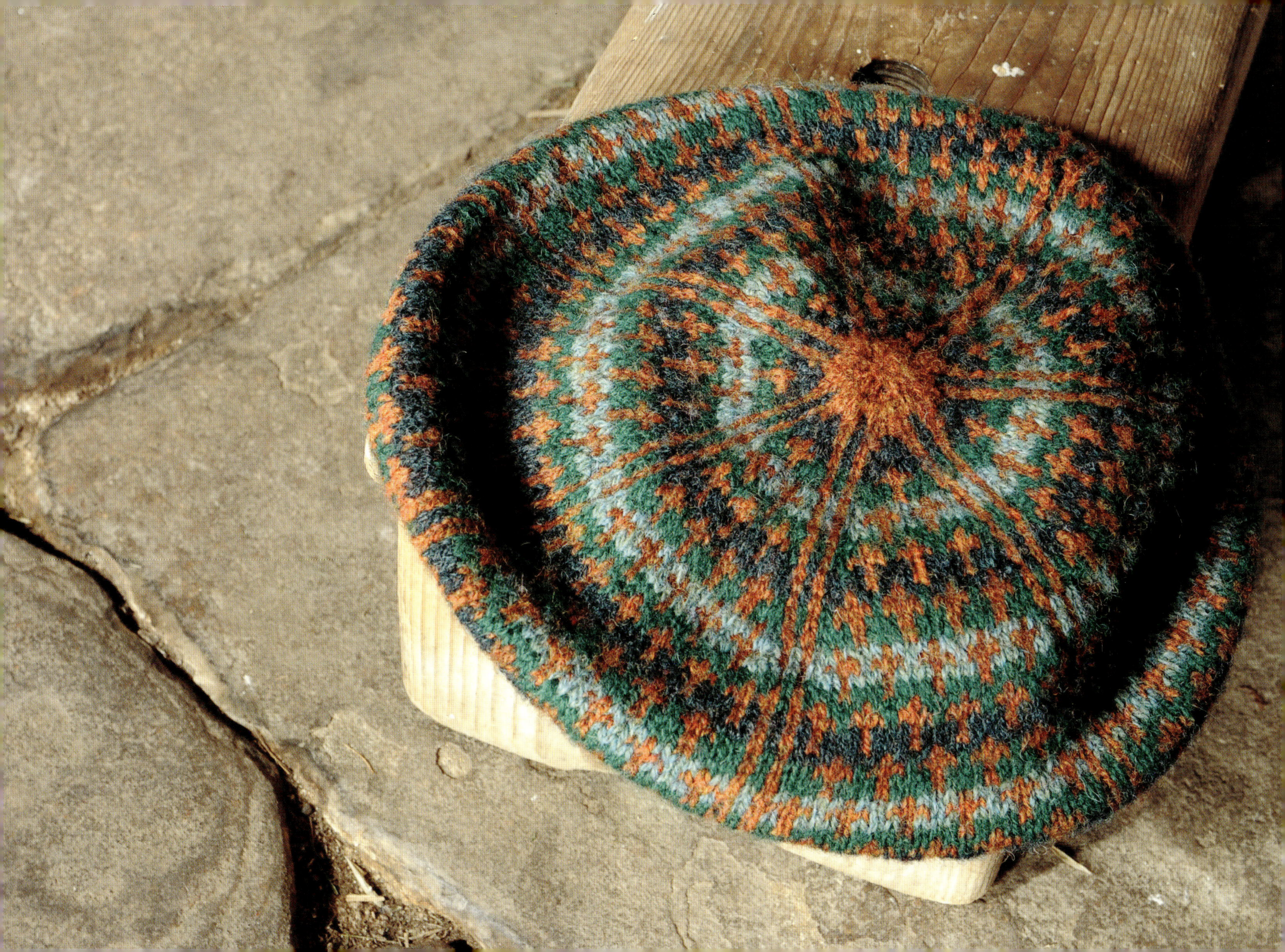

Chart Key

- Yarn A (82); Knit
- Yarn B (34); Knit
- Yarn C (29); Knit
- Yarn D (122); Knit
- Yarn E (FC38); Knit
- Yarn A (82); M1
- Yarn B (34); M1
- Yarn C (29); M1

Chart A

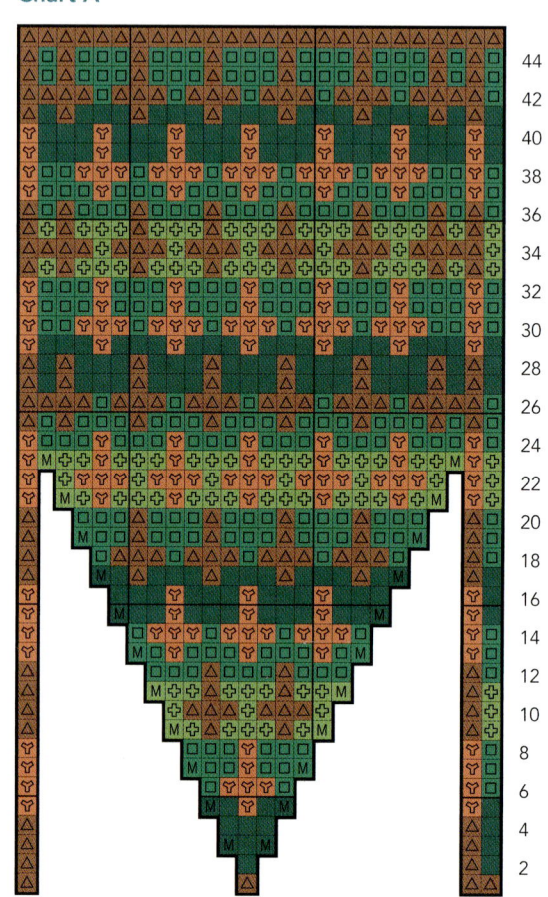

Chart B

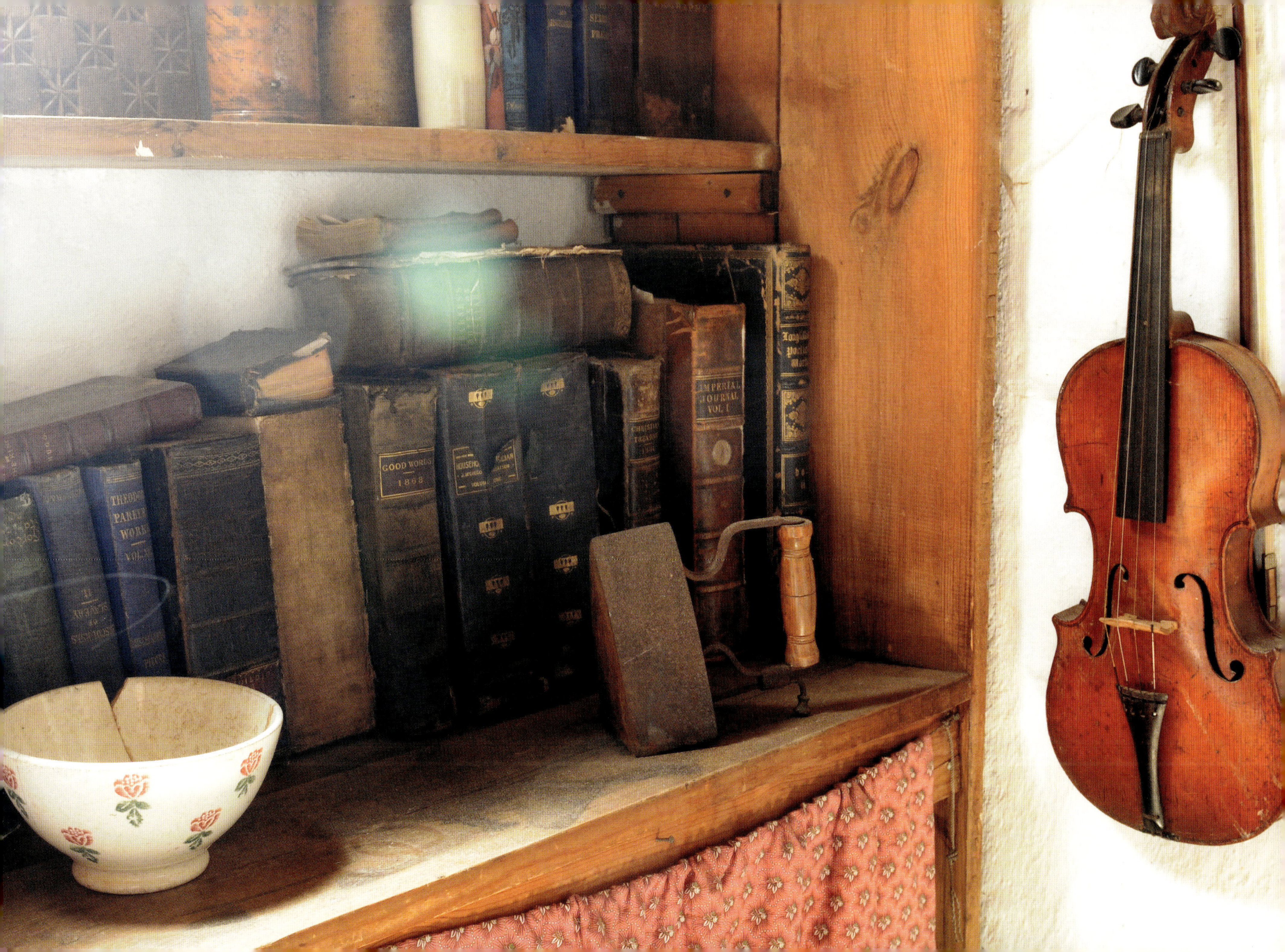
GOOD WORDS
1898
IMPERIAL
JOURNAL
VOL. I

Viking Tunic
designed by Sandra Manson

Materials

Jamieson & Smith Shetland Chunky – 100% Real Shetland Wool (120m/100g balls)

☐ Shade Steekit: 7 (8, 9, 10, 10, 11) x 100g balls

4.5mm (UK 7/US 7) straight needles and a set of DPNs or circular needles in the same size

Waste yarn or stitch holders

Tapestry needle

Sizing

	XS	S	M	L	1X	2X
To fit bust/chest (cm)	81	89	99	107	117	124
(in)	32	35	39	42	46	49
Actual bust/chest (cm)	84	93	102	111	120	129
(in)	33	36.5	40	43.5	47	50.5
Finished length (cm)	61	61	71	71	74	76.5
(in)	24	24	28	28	29	30
Sleeve* (cm)	30	30	32	34	34	34
(in)	12	12	12.5	13.5	13.5	13.5

Size shown in photographs is XS (84cm/33in bust/chest).

*Sleeve is measured from underarm. This top has three-quarter length sleeves.

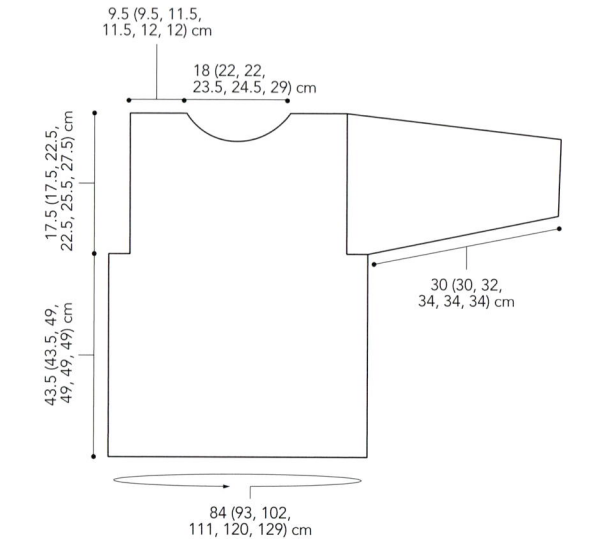

Tension

18 sts & 26 rows = 10cm/4in over st st using 4.5mm needles

Abbreviations

See page 76.

To knit Viking Tunic

Vents

Make 2 alike.

Using 5mm needles, cast on 76 (84, 92, 100, 108, 116) sts.

Row 1 (RS): *K1, P1; rep from * to end of row.

Row 2 (WS): *P1, K1; rep from * to end of row.

These 2 rows set moss st (US seed st). Work in moss stitch for 6 more rows.

Row 9: (K1, P1) twice, knit to last 4 sts, (K1, P1) twice.

Row 10: (P1, K1) twice, purl to last 4 sts, (P1, K1) twice.

These 2 rows set st st with moss st (US seed st) edges. Work as set for 22 more rows.

Leave these stitches on a spare needle, ready to join.

Body

Joining round (RS): Knit across first set of Vent sts, pm, then knit across second set of Vent stitches. 152 (168, 184, 200, 216, 232) sts.

Join to work in the round, taking care not to twist at join between Vents, and place marker for start of round.

Next rnd: Knit.

This round sets st st in the round. Work in st st for 79 (79, 93, 93, 93, 93) more rounds.

Back

†Next row (RS): K5 (5, 5, 8, 10, 10), place these 5 (5, 5, 8, 10, 10) sts on waste yarn or a stitch holder, K66 (74, 82, 84, 88, 96), place next 5 (5, 5, 8, 10, 10) sts on waste yarn or a holder for underarm. Place all sts for Front on waste yarn or on a holder. 66 (74, 82, 84, 88, 96) sts.

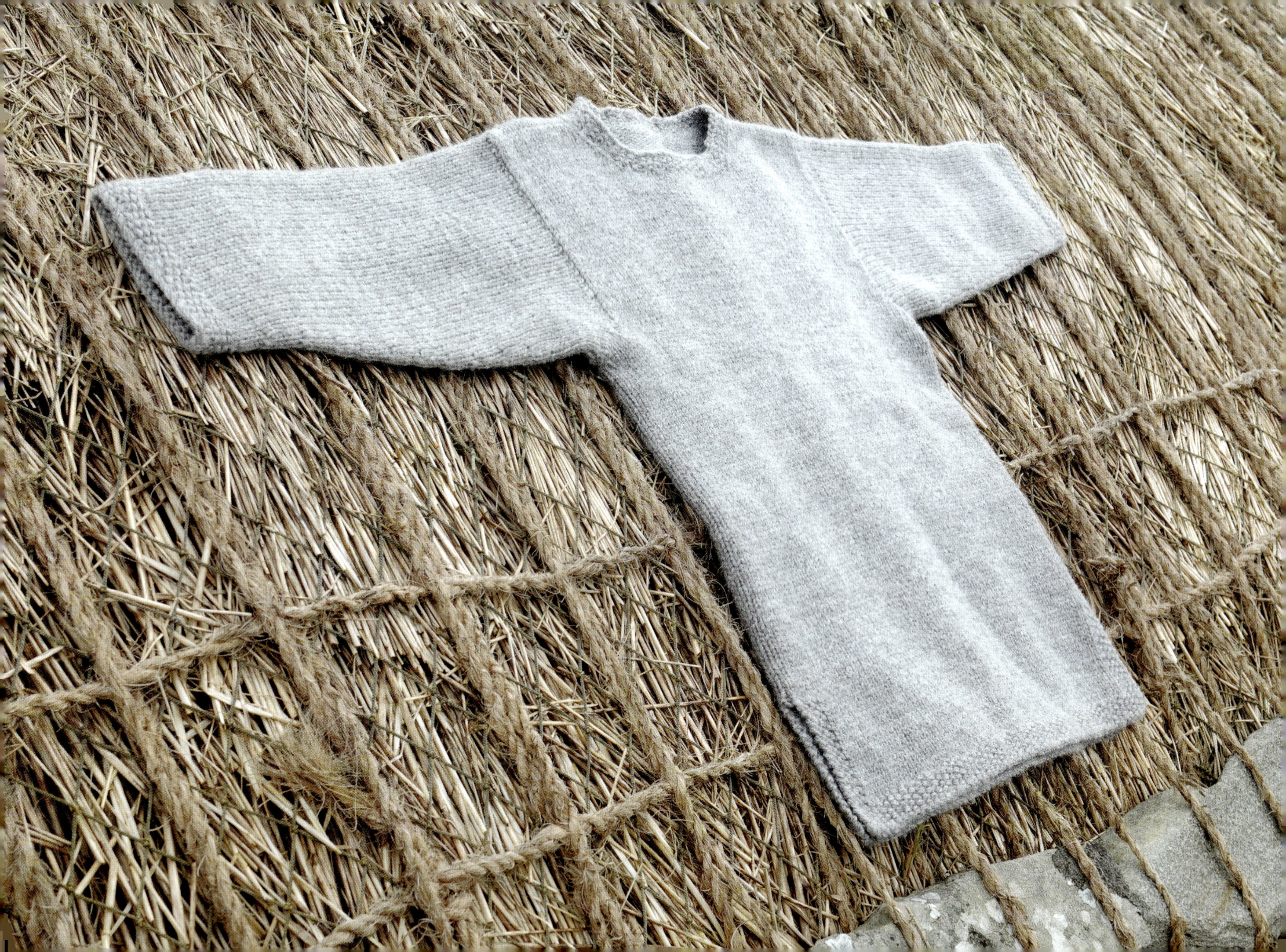

Next row (WS): Purl.

Next row (RS): Knit.†

These 2 rows set st st. Work in st st for 43 (43, 55, 55, 63, 69) more rows, ending with RS facing for next row.

Cast off 17 (17, 21, 21, 22, 22) sts at beginning of the next 2 rows for shoulders.

Leave remaining 32 (40, 40, 42, 44, 52) stitches on a holder for neck.

Front

With RS facing, re-join yarn to sts on hold for Front.

Work from † to † as Back. 66 (74, 82, 84, 88, 96) sts.

Continue in st st for 37 (33, 45, 45, 51, 55) more rows, ending with RS facing for next row.

Next row (RS): K22 (25, 29, 30, 32, 34) and put these sts on holder for left shoulder, K22 (24, 24, 24, 24, 28) and put these on holder for neck, K22 (25, 27, 30, 32, 34), turn and work on these 22 (25, 29, 30, 32, 34) sts only.

Decrease 1 st at neck edge on next 5 (8, 8, 9, 10, 12) rows. 17 (17, 21, 21, 22, 22) sts.

Work 0 (1, 1, 0, 1, 1) row without shaping.

Cast off remaining sts.

With WS facing, re-join yarn to left shoulder sts and complete to match right shoulder.

Sleeves

Make 2 alike.

Cast on 46 (46, 56, 56, 62, 70) sts and join to work in the round, taking care not to twist stitches. Place marker for start of round.

Rnd 1: *K1, P1; rep from * to end of round.

Rnd 2: *P1, K1; rep from * to end of round.

These 2 rounds set moss st in the round. Work in moss st for 6 more rounds.

Next rnd: Knit.

Repeat last round 5 (5, 4, 4, 4, 4) more times

Next rnd: K1, M1, knit to last stitch, M1, K1. 48 (48, 58, 58, 64, 72) sts.

Repeat last 6 (6, 5, 5, 5, 5) rounds 9 (9, 13, 13, 14, 14) more times. 66 (66, 84, 84, 92, 100) sts.

Work straight in st st until sleeve measures 30 (30, 32, 34, 34, 34) cm/12 (12, 12.5, 13.5, 13.5, 13.5) in from cast-on edge.

Next rnd: K5 (5, 5, 8, 10, 10), cast off next 56 (56, 74, 68, 72, 80) sts, leave rem 5 (5, 5, 8, 10, 10) sts unworked.

Join shoulder seams.

Neck

With RS facing, pick up and knit 5 (5, 5, 6, 7, 7) sts down left side of neck, K22 (24, 24, 24, 24, 28) sts from holder for front neck, pick up and knit 5 (5, 5, 6, 7, 7) sts from right side of neck, K32 (40, 40, 42, 44, 52) from holder for back neck. 64 (74, 74, 78, 82, 94) sts.

Join to work in the round.

Rnd 1: *K1, P1; rep from * to end of round.

Rnd 2: *P1, K1; rep from * to end of round.

These 2 rounds set moss st in the round. Work 4 more rounds in moss st.

Cast off.

Making up

Graft sts at underarm of body to sts at sleeve underarm, using Kitchener stitch.

Sew cast-off edge of sleeves neatly in place, easing gently so that shoulder seam matches halfway point along cast-off edge of sleeve.

Wash (see page 79), and dry flat.

BEWARE OF LOW DOORWAYS

Osaka Tea Cosy

designed by Masami Yokoyama

Materials

Jamieson & Smith 2 Ply Jumper Weight – 100% Real Shetland Wool
(118m/25g balls)

- Yarn A – Shade 4: 1 x 25g ball
- Yarn B – Shade 3: 1 x 25g ball
- Yarn C – Shade 9144: 1 x 25g ball
- Yarn D – Shade 43: 1 x 25g ball
- Yarn E – Shade 202: 1 x 25g ball

3mm (UK 11/US 2–3) DPNs (or your preferred needles for small diameter working in the round)

Tapestry needle

Sharp scissors

Sizing

To fit small to medium size teapot. Actual size: 20cm/8in x 28cm/9.5in

Tension

30 sts & 29 rows = 10cm/4in over Fair Isle pattern worked in the round, using 3mm needles

Abbreviations

See page 76.

To knit Osaka Tea Cosy

Body

Using 3mm needles and yarn A, cast on 144 sts. Join to work in the round, taking care not to twist sts and place marker for start of round. If using DPNs, distribute sts evenly over needles.

Rnd 1: Work from chart A, repeating the 72 sts shown twice.

Work from chart A until round 14 is complete.

Rnd 15: Using yarn E Sl 1, K1, psso, then work in pattern from chart for 70 sts, using yarn E K2tog, then work in pattern from chart to end of round. 142 sts.

Rnd 16: *Using the backwards loop method and yarn B, cast on 12 sts for the steek, work in pattern from chart for 71 sts; rep from * once more. 166 sts (including 24 steek sts).

Work from chart A until round 44 is complete.

Rnd 45: *Cast off 12 sts, work in pattern until you have 71 sts on right-hand needle after cast-off sts; rep from * once more. 142 sts.

Rnd 46: *Using yarn E M1, K71; repeat from * once more. 144 sts.

Rnd 47: Using yarn E K144.

Top

Partial rnd: Remove start of round marker, using yarn E K10, place new start of round marker.

Rnd 1: Now work from chart B, repeating the motif 6 times in each round. 132 sts.

Continue to work from chart B, working decreases as shown on the chart on alternate rounds, until round 21 is complete. 12 sts.

Break yarn and pass through remaining stitches and fasten off carefully. Darn in all ends

Making up

Using sharp scissors, cut up the centre of the steeks, fold in the edges and slip-stitch them neatly to the wrong side.

Wash (see page 79) and then block over a pudding basin, or similar shaped object, thus allowing the colourwork stitches to settle and even out.

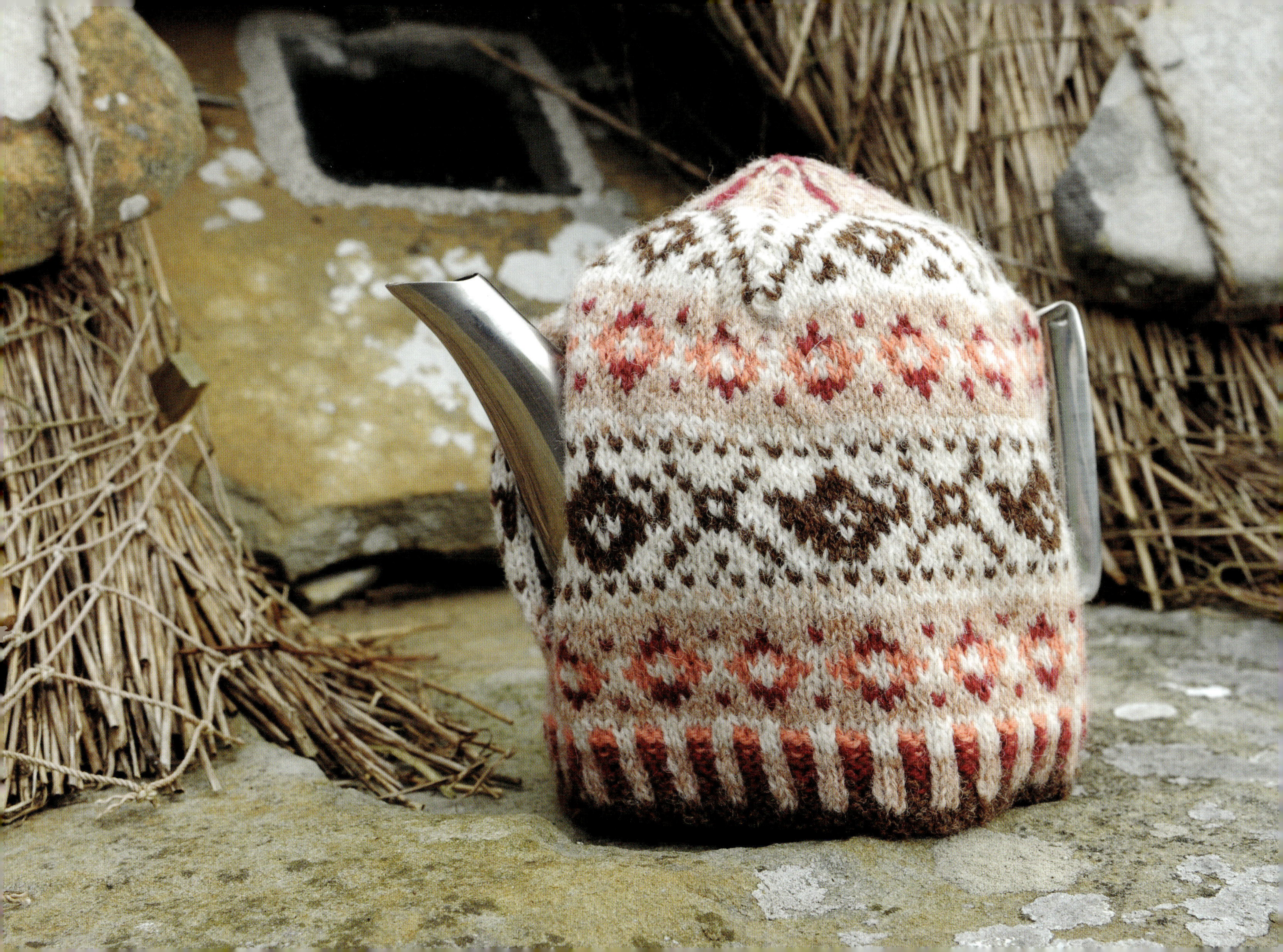

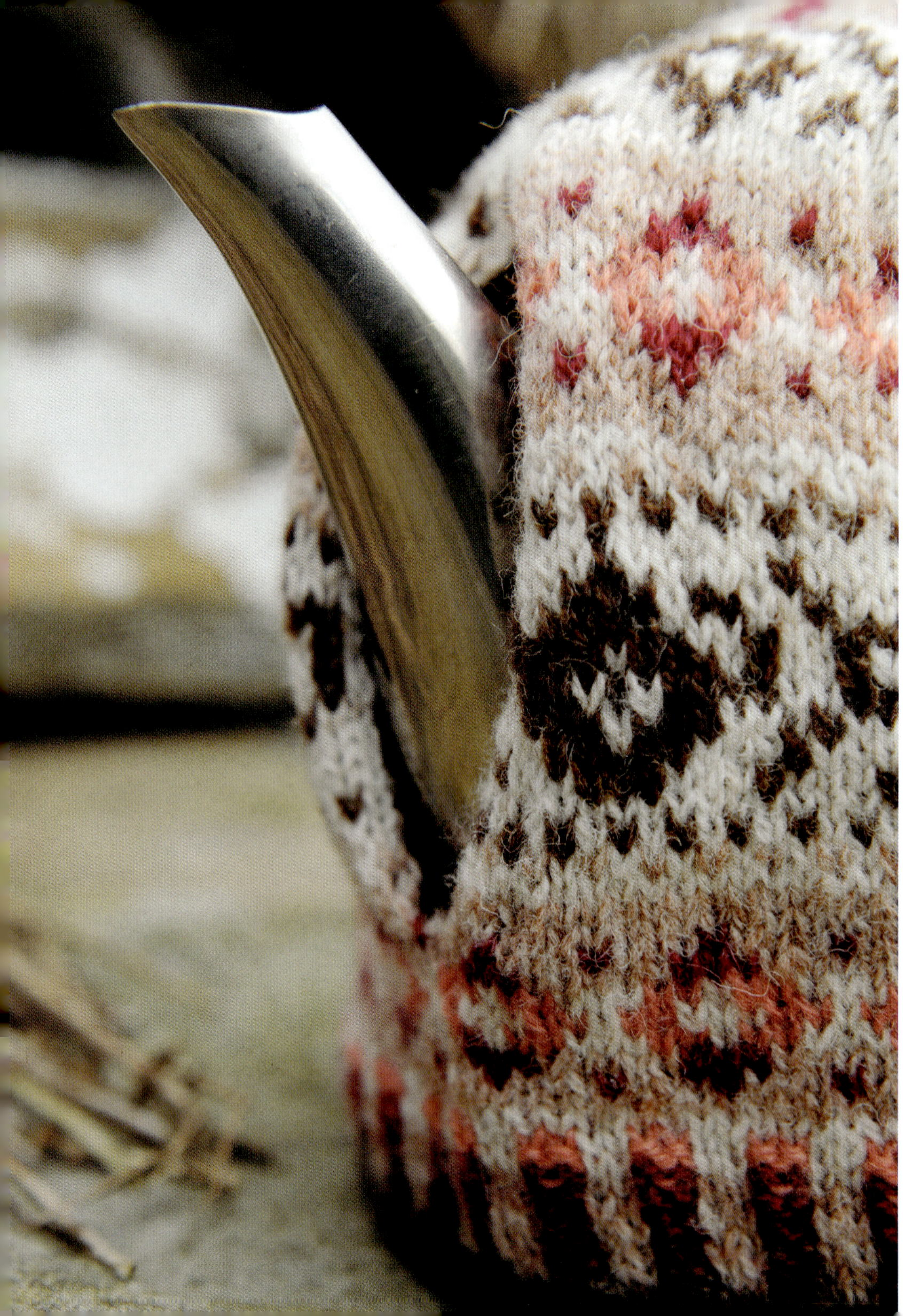
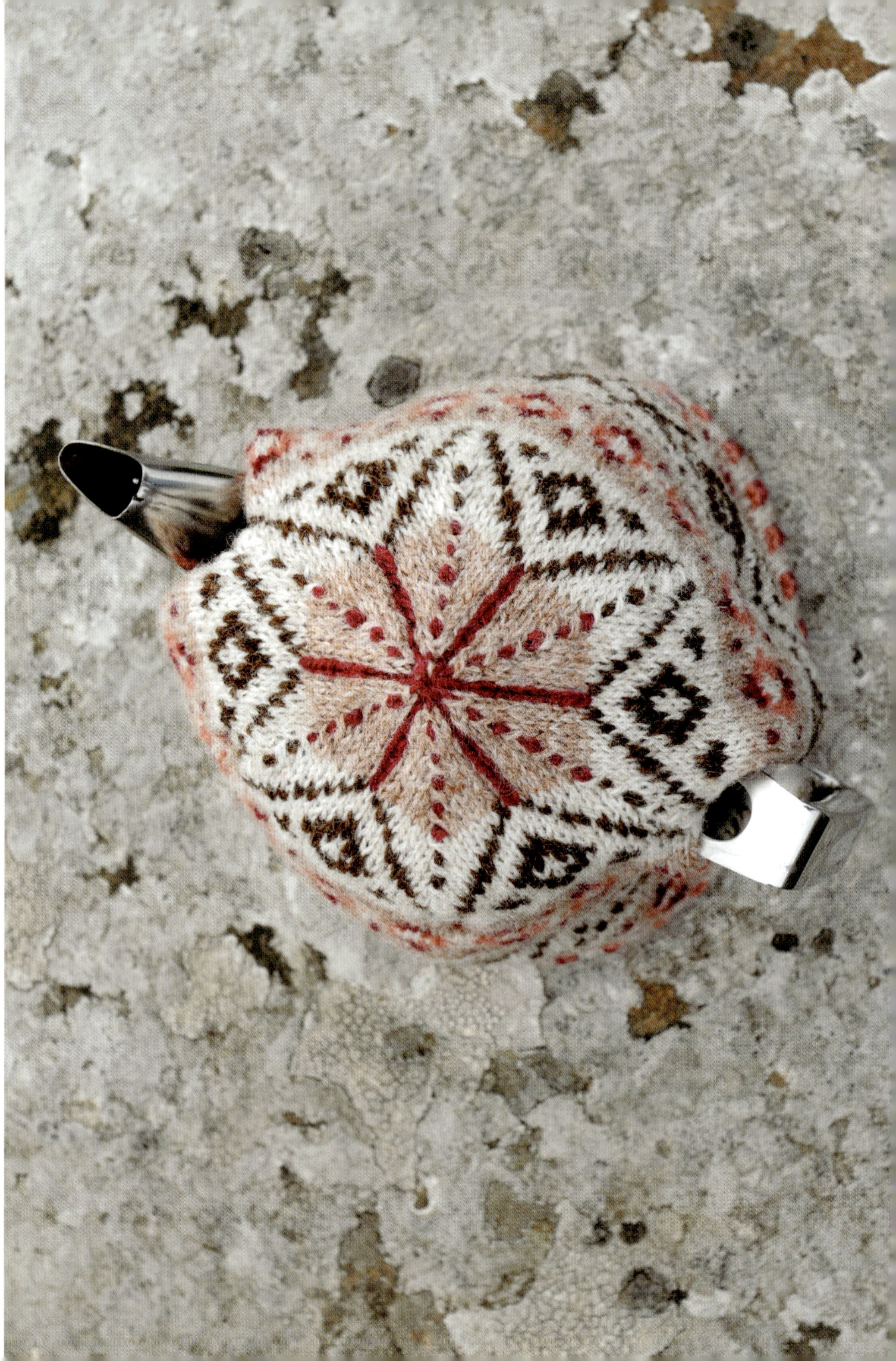

Chart A

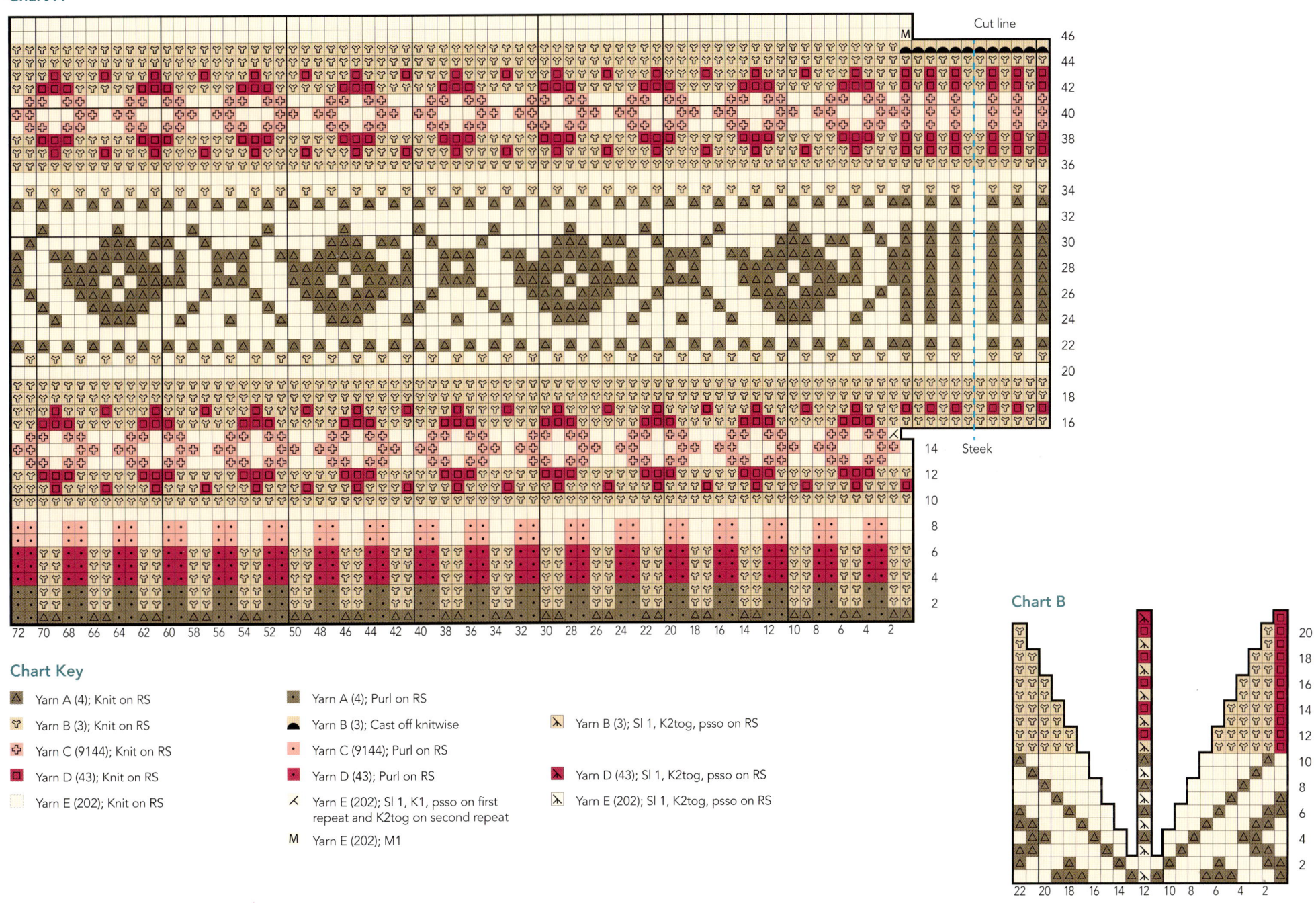

Cut line

Steek

Chart B

Chart Key

- ▲ Yarn A (4); Knit on RS
- ⊻ Yarn B (3); Knit on RS
- ✚ Yarn C (9144); Knit on RS
- ▢ Yarn D (43); Knit on RS
- ▫ Yarn E (202); Knit on RS
- ▪ Yarn A (4); Purl on RS
- ⏝ Yarn B (3); Cast off knitwise
- • Yarn C (9144); Purl on RS
- • Yarn D (43); Purl on RS
- ⟋ Yarn E (202); Sl 1, K1, psso on first repeat and K2tog on second repeat
- M Yarn E (202); M1
- ⟍ Yarn B (3); Sl 1, K2tog, psso on RS
- ⟍ Yarn D (43); Sl 1, K2tog, psso on RS
- ⟍ Yarn E (202); Sl 1, K2tog, psso on RS

Kergord Scarf
designed by Mary Kay

Materials
Jamieson & Smith Shetland Supreme 1 Ply Lace Weight – 100% Real Shetland Wool (400m/25g balls)

☐ Shade White: 2 x 25g balls

2.5mm (UK 13–12/US 1–2) needles

Tapestry needle

Sizing
Scarf 25cm x 118cm/10in x 46.5in, after dressing

Tension
34 sts & 50 rows = 10cm/4in over lace pattern using 2.5mm needles, after dressing

Abbreviations
See page 76.

Pattern notes
The length of the scarf can be adjusted by increasing or decreasing the number of times rows 98 – 113 are repeated.

The scarf is worked on a garter stitch background, so it is reversible. RS and WS rows are hard to distinguish, and at different points in the pattern, the lace is worked on both RS and WS rows. If you want to be able to tell the difference between the sides of the scarf, then a small loop of fine, coloured waste thread attached to the RS of the work will be helpful.

To knit Kergord Scarf

First part
Using 2.5mm needles and the knitted-on or lace method, cast on 85 sts.

Row 1 (RS): Work from row 1 of chart A, reading from right to left.

Row 2 (WS): Work from row 2 of chart A, reading from left to right.

Continue to work from chart as set until row 87 is complete. Read all RS rows from right to left, and all WS rows from left to right.

Break yarn and leave these sts on a spare needle or stitch holder.

Second part
Using 2.5mm needles and the knitted-on or lace method, cast on 85 sts.

Work from chart A as set previously, until row 113 is complete.

Repeat rows 98 to 113 (inclusive) 20 more times.

Now work all 16 rows from chart B (row 1 is WS, so don't forget to read from left to right).

Return the 85 sts from the first half of the scarf to a needle. Hold the two halves of the scarf with WS facing each other and graft the two pieces of knitting together using Kitchener stitch.

Finishing
Darn in any ends but do not trim.

Dress the scarf as follows:

Fold the scarf in half so that both cast-on edges meet. Using cotton thread, sew the side edges together picking up the longer sts between the 'ridges', making a tube which is half the length of the scarf. Cut a piece of cardboard to about one-fifth wider than the width of the scarf and more than one-fifth longer than the tube (this can be trimmed later).

Wash (see page 79). Pull the tube over the cardboard, stretching gently. Shorten the length of the cardboard if necessary and sew the points of the matching peaks together. Leave to dry and remove cotton thread, and trim any ends.

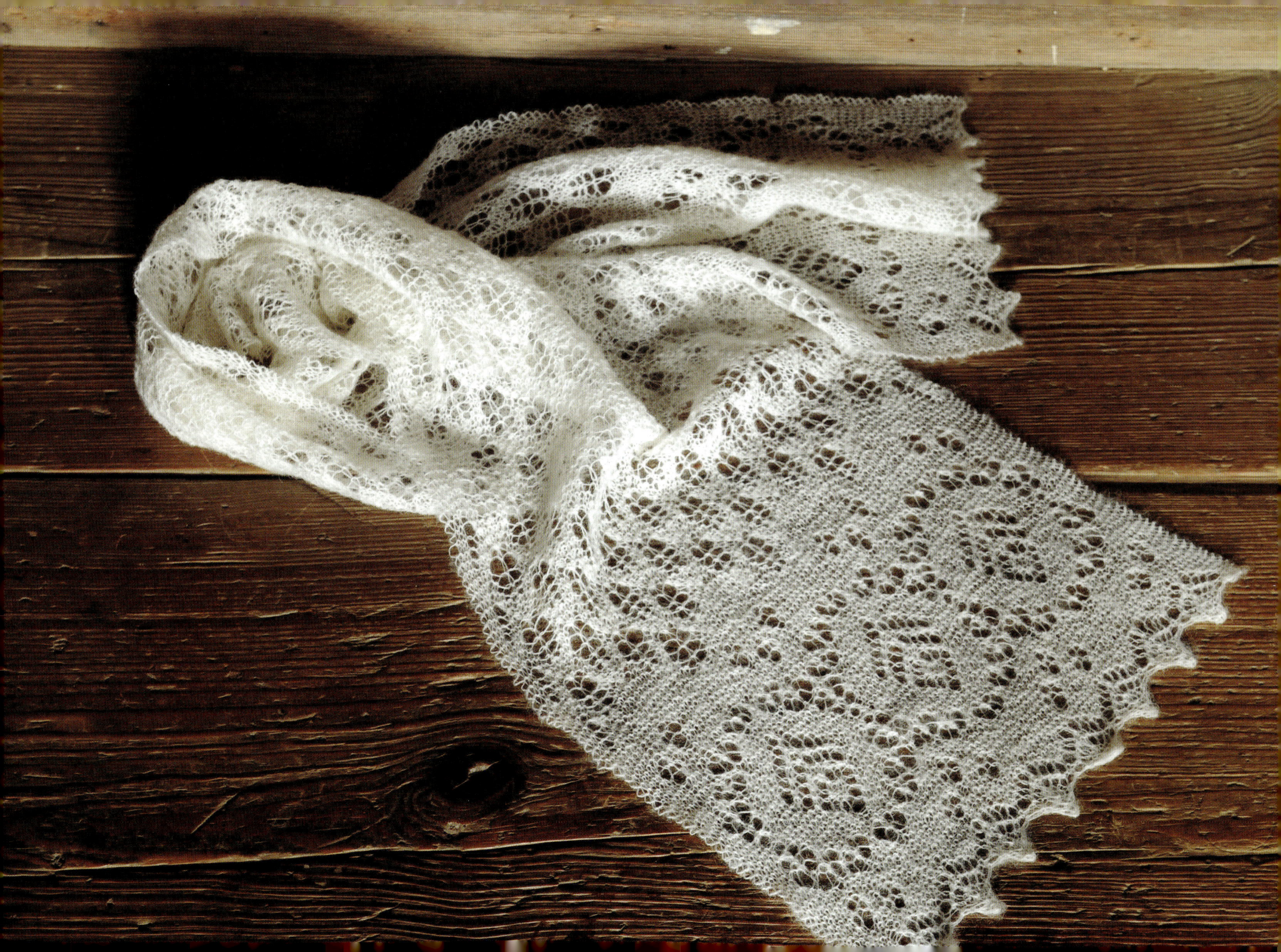

Chart Key

- ☐ Knit on RS, Purl on WS
- ▨ Purl on RS, Knit on WS
- O Yarnover
- ╲ Sl 1, K1, psso on RS
- ╲ Sl 1, K1, psso on WS
- ╱ K2tog on RS
- ╱ K2tog on WS
- ⋌ Sl 1, K2tog, psso on RS
- ⋌ Sl 1, K2tog, psso on WS
- ☐ Pattern repeat
- ▓ Tinted area shows previous row for reference only. Do not knit.

Chart A

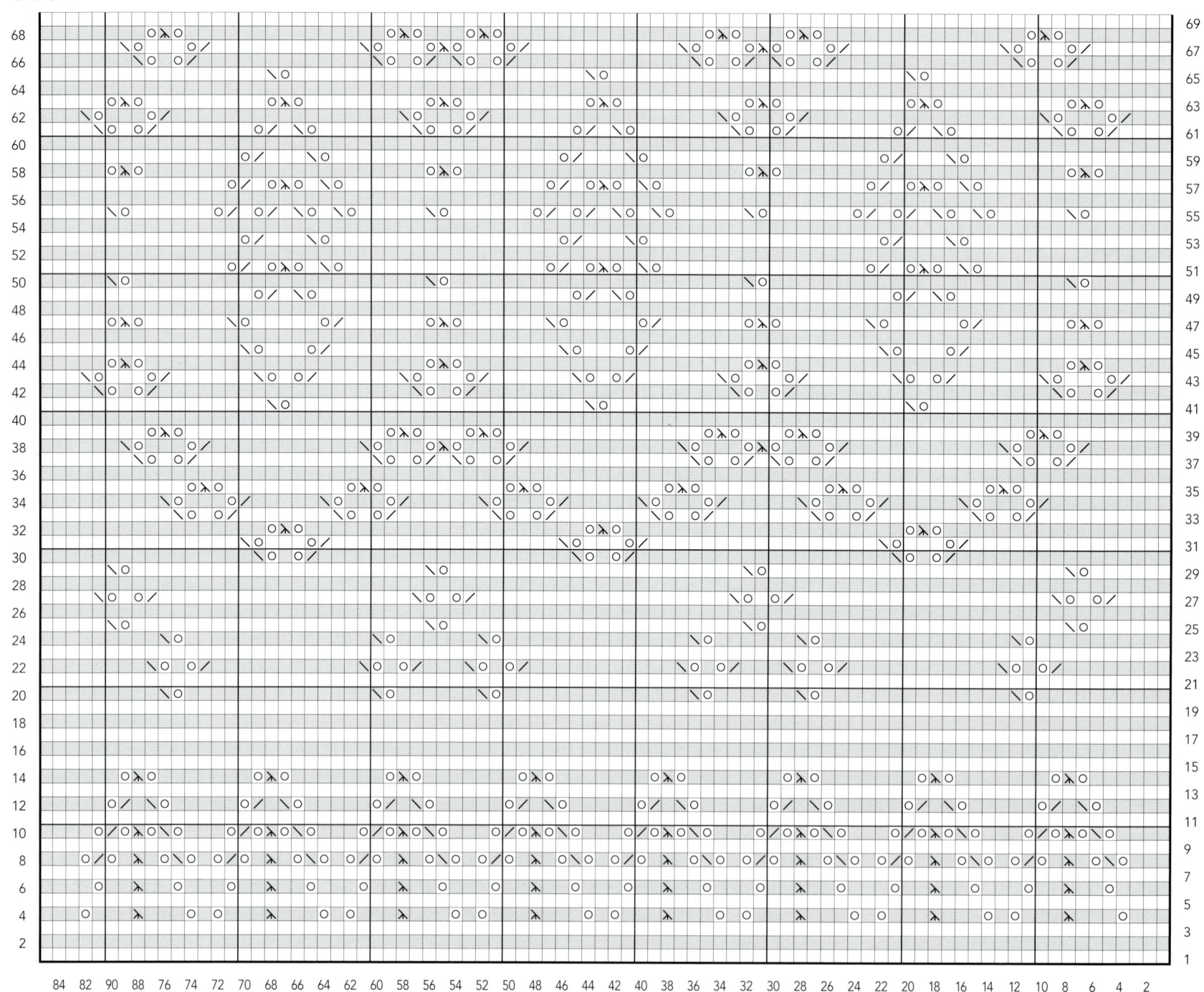

Chart B (Row 1 is WS)

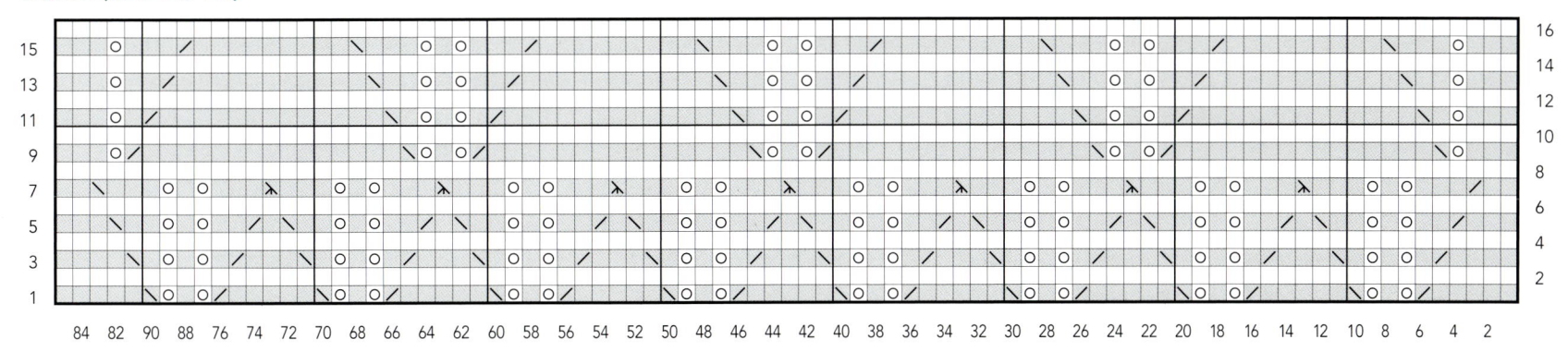

Chart A continued

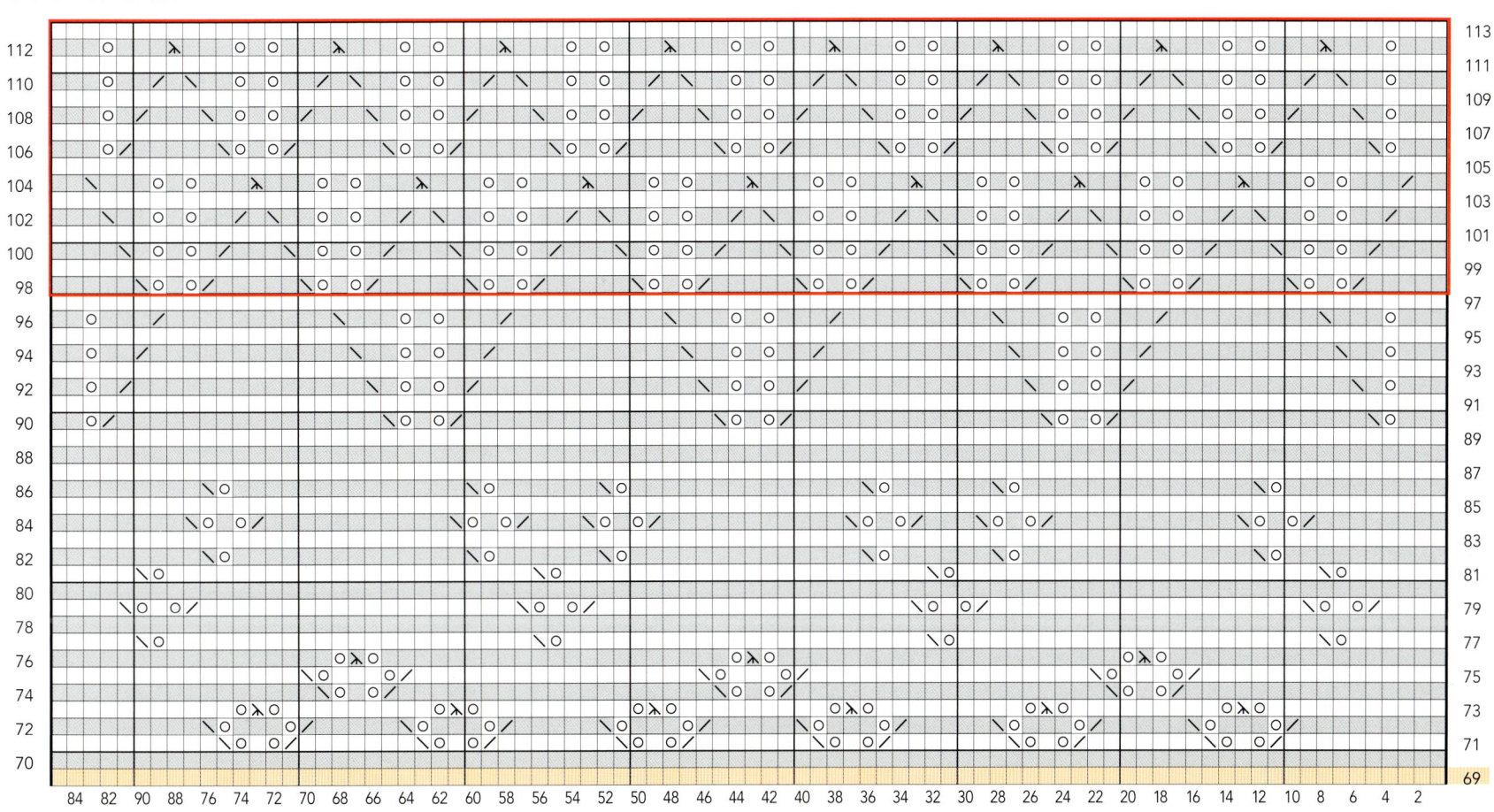

Melby Jumper Dress

designed by Gudrun Johnston

Materials

Jamieson & Smith 2 Ply Jumper Weight – 100% Real Shetland Wool (118m/25g balls)

- Yarn A – Shade 4: 5 (5, 6, 6, 7, 8, 8, 9) x 25g balls
- Yarn B – Shade 9097: 1 (1, 1, 1, 1, 2, 2, 2) x 25g ball
- Yarn C – Shade FC38: 1 (1, 1, 1, 1, 2, 2, 2) x 25g ball
- Yarn D – Shade 9113: 1 (1, 1, 1, 1, 2, 2, 2) x 25g ball
- Yarn E – Shade 72: 1 (1, 1, 1, 1, 2, 2, 2) x 25g ball
- Yarn F – Shade FC55: 1 (1, 1, 1, 1, 2, 2, 2) x 25g ball

3.5mm (UK 10–9/US 4) circular needle, 60cm/24in long
3.5mm (UK 10–9/US 4) circular needle, 40cm/16in long
3.5mm (UK 10–9/US 4) set of DPNs
3.25mm (UK 10/US 3) circular needle, 40cm/16in long

Sizing

	3XS	XXS	XS	S	M	L	XL	XXL
To fit bust (cm)	71	76	79	84	89	94	99	104
(in)	28	30	31	33	35	37	39	41
Actual bust (cm)	71.5	76.5	80	85	90	95	100	105
(in)	28.5	30	31.5	33.5	35.5	37.5	39.5	41.5
Actual length* (cm)	58	58	60	60	61	64	66	70
(in)	23	23	23.5	23.5	24	25	26	27.5

Size shown in photographs is 3XS (71.5cm/28.5in bust).

Tension

24 sts and 38 rows = 10cm/4in over st st using 3.5mm needles

Abbreviations

See page 76.

Pattern notes

Dress is designed to reach top of thigh, and to be worn over trousers or leggings.

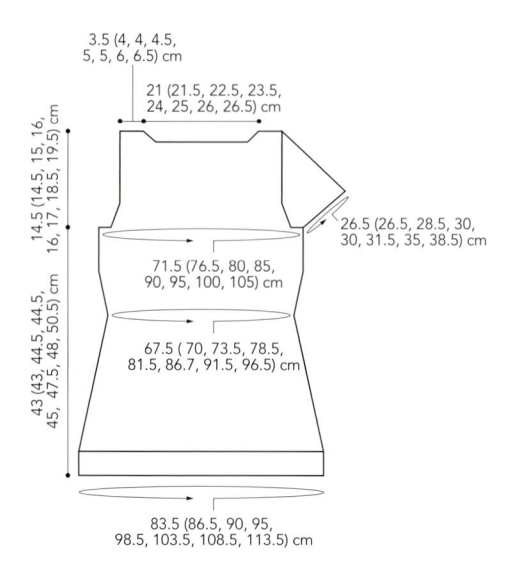

To create stripe sequence:

Work 2 rounds yarn B, 2 rounds yarn A, 2 rounds yarn C, 2 rounds yarn A, 2 rounds yarn D, 2 rounds yarn A, 2 rounds yarn E, 2 rounds yarn A, 2 rounds shade F, 2 rounds yarn A.

Repeat this 20 round (row) stripe pattern as indicated.

To knit Melby Jumper Dress

Hem

Using 3.5mm circular needle (60cm/24in long) and yarn A, cast on 200 (208, 216, 228, 236, 248, 260, 272) sts, place marker and join for working in the round.

Rnd 1: *K2, P2; repeat from * to end of round.

Last round sets 2 x 2 rib, continue working in rib for a total of 32 rounds.

Body

Begin working stripe sequence (see pattern notes), beginning with yarn B, and knit 7 rounds (now working in st st). **At the same time**, place a marker after 100 (104, 108, 114, 118, 124, 130, 136) sts

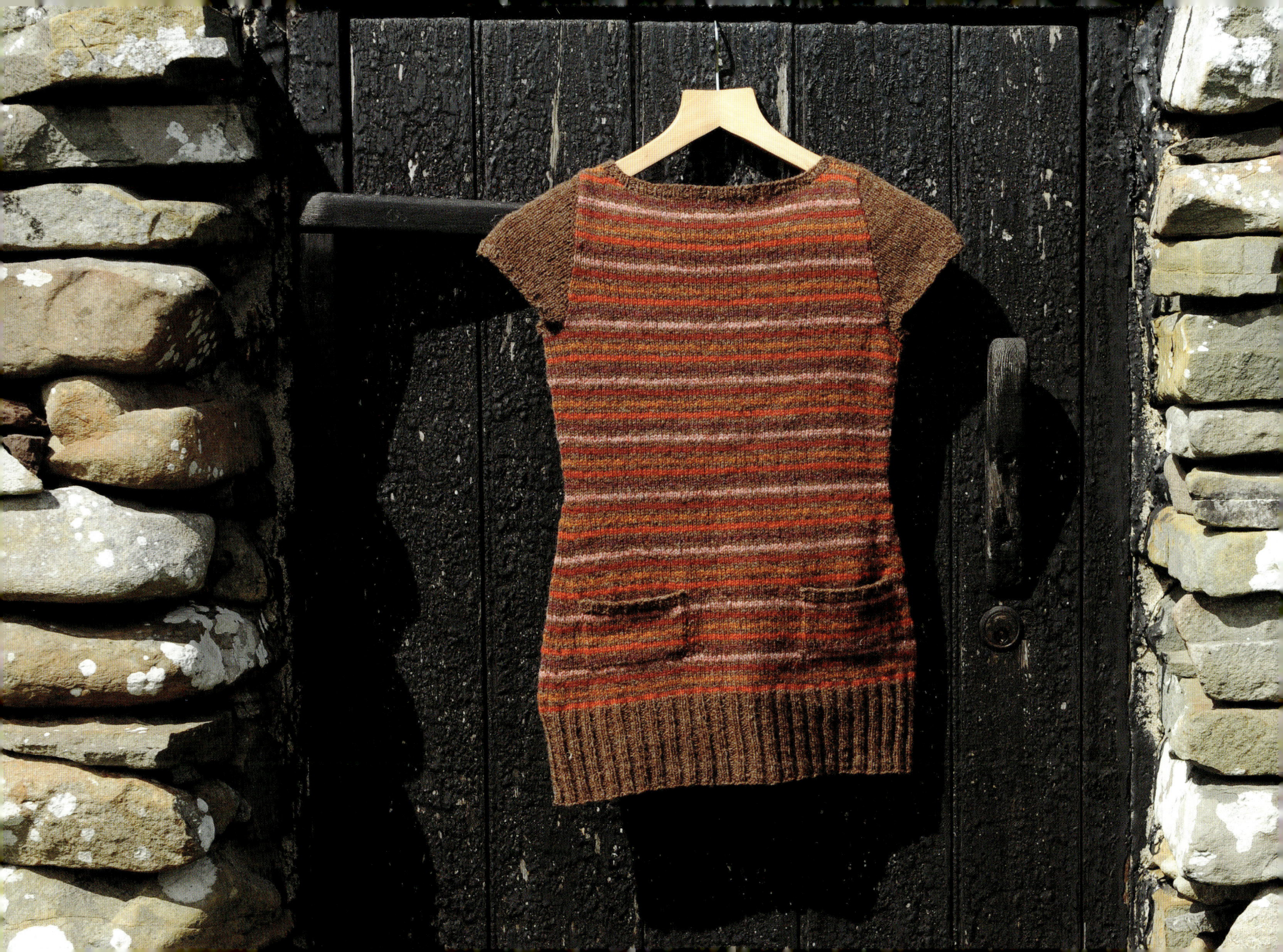

for side seam shaping.

Rnd 8 (dec): *K1, K2tog, knit to 3 sts before next marker, SSK, K1, slip marker; repeat from * once more. 196 (204, 212, 224, 232, 244, 256, 268) sts.

Knit 6 more rounds without shaping.

Rnd 15 (pocket placement): K11 (13, 15, 14, 16, 15, 16, 18) sts, place next 26 (26, 26, 30, 30, 34, 34, 34) sts on waste yarn for pocket, cast on 26 (26, 26, 30, 30, 34, 34, 34) sts, K24 (24, 24, 24, 24, 24, 28, 30), place next 26 (26, 26, 30, 30, 34, 34, 34) sts on holder for second pocket, cast on 26 (26, 26, 30, 30, 34, 34, 34) sts, work to end as normal.

Continue working in st st, following stripe sequence, and work dec round (as round 8) on next and 4 foll 8th rounds, then on every 6th round 4 times. 160 (168, 176, 188, 196, 208, 220, 232) sts.

Work even in st st for another 11 (11, 13, 13, 15, 15, 17, 17) rounds.

Inc rnd: *K1, M1L, knit to 1 st before marker, M1R, K1, slm; rep from * once more. 164 (172, 180, 192, 200, 212, 224, 236) sts.

Repeat inc round every 14th (10th, 10th, 10th, 8th, 10th, 10th, 12th) round 2 (3, 3, 3, 4, 4, 4, 4) more times. 172 (184, 192, 204, 216, 228, 240, 252) sts.

Work even in st st for 20 (18, 20, 20, 18, 20, 20, 22) more rounds. Break yarn, leaving a tail.

Divide for front and back

Place last 5 (5, 5, 6, 6, 7, 7, 8) sts before beginning of round marker and first 5 (5, 5, 6, 6, 7, 7, 8) sts of round on waste yarn for underarm, leaving marker in place.

Re-join yarn (still following stripe sequence) and knit across 76 (82, 86, 90, 96, 100, 106, 110) sts of front, place next 10 (10, 10, 12, 12, 14, 14, 16) sts on waste yarn for underarm and then place remaining 76 (82, 86, 90, 96, 100, 106, 110) sts on separate waste yarn for back.

Continuing on front sts, turn work to WS and purl 1 row.

Shape armhole

Dec row: K1, SSK, knit to last 3 sts, K2tog, K1. 74 (80, 84, 88, 94, 98, 104, 108) sts.

Continue in st st, now working back and forth in rows, and repeat decrease row every 4th row 4 (5, 5, 5, 6, 7, 7, 7) more times. 66 (70, 74, 78, 82, 84, 90, 94) sts.

Continue in st st until a total of 48 (48, 50, 52, 52, 56, 62, 66) rows have been worked from beginning of front.

Shape neck

The neck is shaped using a bias cast-off method, please read foll instructions carefully.

Left neck edge

First row: K14 (15, 16, 17, 18, 18, 20, 21), turn work and bring yarn to front, slip the first st on the left-hand needle to the right-hand needle then *pass the 2nd st on the right-hand needle over the stitch just slipped (1 st has been cast off), purl next st and then repeat from * twice more to cast off a total of 3 sts, purl to end.

Second row: K11 (12, 13, 14, 15, 15, 17, 18) and work bias cast off as before but only cast off 2 sts, purl to end.

Third row: K9 (10, 11, 12, 13, 13, 15, 16) and work bias cast off as before, again only cast off 2 sts, purl to end. 8 (9, 10, 11, 12, 12, 14, 15) sts.

Work 2 more rows in st st.

Cut yarn and place 8 (9, 10, 11, 12, 12, 14, 15) sts of left shoulder on waste yarn.

Place 36 (38, 40, 42, 44, 46, 48, 50) sts of centre front on waste yarn.

Right neck edge

Re-join yarn to armhole edge of right front, ready to begin a WS row.

First row: P14 (15, 16, 17, 18, 18, 20, 21), turn work, take yarn to back of work, slip the first st on the left-hand needle to the right-hand needle then * pass the 2nd st on the right-hand needle over the stitch just slipped (1 st has been cast off), knit next st and then repeat from * twice more to cast off a total of 3 sts, knit to end.

Second row: P11 (12, 13, 14, 15, 15, 17, 18) and work bias cast off as before but only cast off 2 sts, knit to end.

Third row: P9 (10, 11, 12, 13, 13, 15, 16) sts and work bias cast off as before, again only cast off 2 sts, knit to end. 8 (9, 10, 11, 12, 12, 14, 15) sts.

Work 2 more rows in st st. Cut yarn and place 8 (9, 10, 11, 12, 12, 14, 15) sts of right shoulder on waste yarn.

Back

Place 76 (82, 86, 90, 96, 100, 106, 110) held sts of back onto the needles and re-join yarn ready to begin a RS row.

Work 2 rows in st st. Complete as for front, beginning at the 1st decrease row to shape armholes.

Join shoulders

Place both sets of sts for left shoulder onto separate 3.5mm DPNs. Holding the left back shoulder sts and left front shoulder sts with right sides facing, join sts using the three-needle cast off as foll:

Using a third needle, knit together the first stitch from each needle. *Knit together the next stitch from each needle. You will now have 2 sts on right-hand needle, cast off 1 st in the normal way. Rep from * until all of the shoulder sts have been cast off. Break yarn and fasten off.

Repeat the shoulder join with the right front shoulder and right back shoulder sts.

Sleeves

Work alike on both sides.

The sleeves are worked by picking up sts from the armhole and working short rows to shape the sleeve cap. The ratio for picking up sts around the armhole is about 1 stitch out of every 2 rows or 1 stitch per stripe.

Using 3.5mm circular needles (40cm/16in long), with RS facing place the 5 (5, 5, 6, 6, 7, 7, 8) sts to the left of the underarm marker on the needles. Re-join yarn A and knit across these sts, next pick up and knit 27 (27, 29, 30, 30, 31, 35, 38) sts to shoulder join, place marker, pick up and knit 27 (27, 29, 30, 30, 31, 35, 38) sts down the other side to where the rest of the underarm sts are being held, place these 5 (5, 5, 6, 6, 7, 7, 8) sts to the right of the marker onto the left-hand needle tip and knit across. 64 (64, 68, 72, 72, 76, 84, 92) sts.

Place marker for working in the round.

Short row shaping
Row 1 (RS): Knit to 5 sts past shoulder seam marker, w&t.

Row 2 (WS): Purl to 5 sts past shoulder seam marker, w&t.

Repeat rows 1 and 2 making the w&t one more st past the previously made w&t each time until all sts except the underarm sts have been worked.

After the last w&t, knit to end of round.

Next rnd: *K2, P2; repeat from * to end.

Repeat this round twice more. Cast off all sts in rib.

Neckband
Using the 3.25mm circular needles (40cm/16in long) and yarn A, starting at the join of the left shoulder with RS facing, pick up and knit 8 sts down to held front neck sts, place these 36 (38, 40, 42, 44, 46, 48, 50) sts on a spare needle and knit across them, pick up and knit 8 sts to right shoulder join, then 8 sts down to held back neck sts, place these 36 (38, 40, 42, 44, 46, 48, 50) sts onto a spare needle and knit across them, pick up and knit 8 more sts to left shoulder join. Place marker and join for working in the round. 104 (108, 112, 116, 120, 124, 128, 132) sts.

Rnd 1: *K2, P2; rep from * to end of round.

Repeat last round twice more. Cast off all sts in rib.

Pockets
Work both pockets alike. Place 26 (26, 26, 30, 30, 34, 34, 34) held sts of pocket onto 3.5mm needle. Re-join yarn in stripe sequence and work 22 rows in striped st st.

NB: If you prefer a deeper pocket work more rows in stocking st.

Row 1: *K2, P2; repeat from * to last 2 sts, K2.

Row 2: *P2, K2; repeat from * to last 2 sts, P2.

Repeat row 1 once more. Cast off all sts in rib.

Finishing
Slip-stitch down the sides of the pockets. Darn in all ends. Wash (see page 79) and lay garment out on a dry towel to measurements for your size, making sure the ribbing at hem is more relaxed.

Wool Brokers Socks

designed by Lesley Smith

Materials

Jamieson & Smith Shetland Supreme 2 Ply Jumper Weight – 100% Real Shetland Wool (172m/50g balls)

- Yarn A – Gaulmogot (2006): 2 x 50g balls

Jamieson & Smith 2 Ply Jumper Weight – 100% Real Shetland Wool (118m/25g balls)

- Yarn B – Shade FC14: 1x 25g ball
- Yarn C – Shade FC56: 1 x 25g ball
- Yarn D – Shade 133: 1 x 25g ball
- Yarn E – Shade 72: 1 x 25g ball

3mm (UK 11/US 2–3) DPNs (or your preferred needles for small diameter working in the round)

Sizing

Ladies Medium

Ankle circumference: 24cm/9.5in

Foot length: 24cm/9.5in

Tension

34 sts & 36 rows = 10cm/4in over Fair Isle pattern using 3mm needles

Abbreviations

See page 76.

Pattern notes

These socks do not require stitches to be grafted together.

Distribute stitches around your needles as you find most comfortable. To avoid getting ladders in your work where you change from one needle to the next, it is a good idea to move where the needle change occurs every few rounds. If you have difficulty keeping the fabric from bunching at the needle changes, then try turning the sock inside out as you knit it. This will help to keep the stitches even, and prevent the floats of yarn at the rear of the work from getting too tight. When the yarn not in use is carried at the rear of the work for 5 sts or longer, it is best to weave the yarn in once along the back of the knitting.

The waste yarn for the heel should be in a contrasting shade and of a similar weight to that of the other yarns used. Using a synthetic waste yarn can make it easier to remove later.

To knit Wool Brokers Socks

Cuff

Using 3mm needles, cast on 72 sts in yarn A using the long-tail cast-on method. Join to work in the round, taking care not to twist sts. Place marker for start of round.

Divide sts evenly over your chosen needles.

Rnd 1: Working from chart A, repeat 4-stitch motif 18 times in each round, and reading all chart rows from right to left.

Last round sets chart A pattern. Continue to work from chart A until round 13 is complete.

Leg

Rnd 14: Using yarn A only, *K7, M1; repeat from * to last 2 sts, K2. 82 sts.

Rnd 15: Work from chart B row 1, repeating the 41-stitch motif twice in each round.

Rnd 15 sets chart B pattern. Continue to work from chart B until row 45 of chart is complete.

Heel insert

Next rnd: Work first 41 sts of round from row 46 of chart B. Don't break yarn A. Using waste yarn, K41, then break waste yarn and return to start of these 41 sts. Using yarn A only, knit these 41 stitches again. You will now have 41 sts of waste yarn in your fabric. After the completion of the foot, you will come back to these stitches, unpick the waste yarn, and work an 'afterthought' heel.

Foot

Next rnd: Work 41 sts following row 47 of chart B, *K1A, K1D; rep from * to last stitch, K1A.

Last round sets chart B pattern on top of foot, and stripes on sole of foot. Use the same colours for the stripe pattern as you have been using on the top of the foot (so change from yarn D to yarn C when working row 50 of chart B). Continue to work from chart B as set, until row 87 of chart is complete.

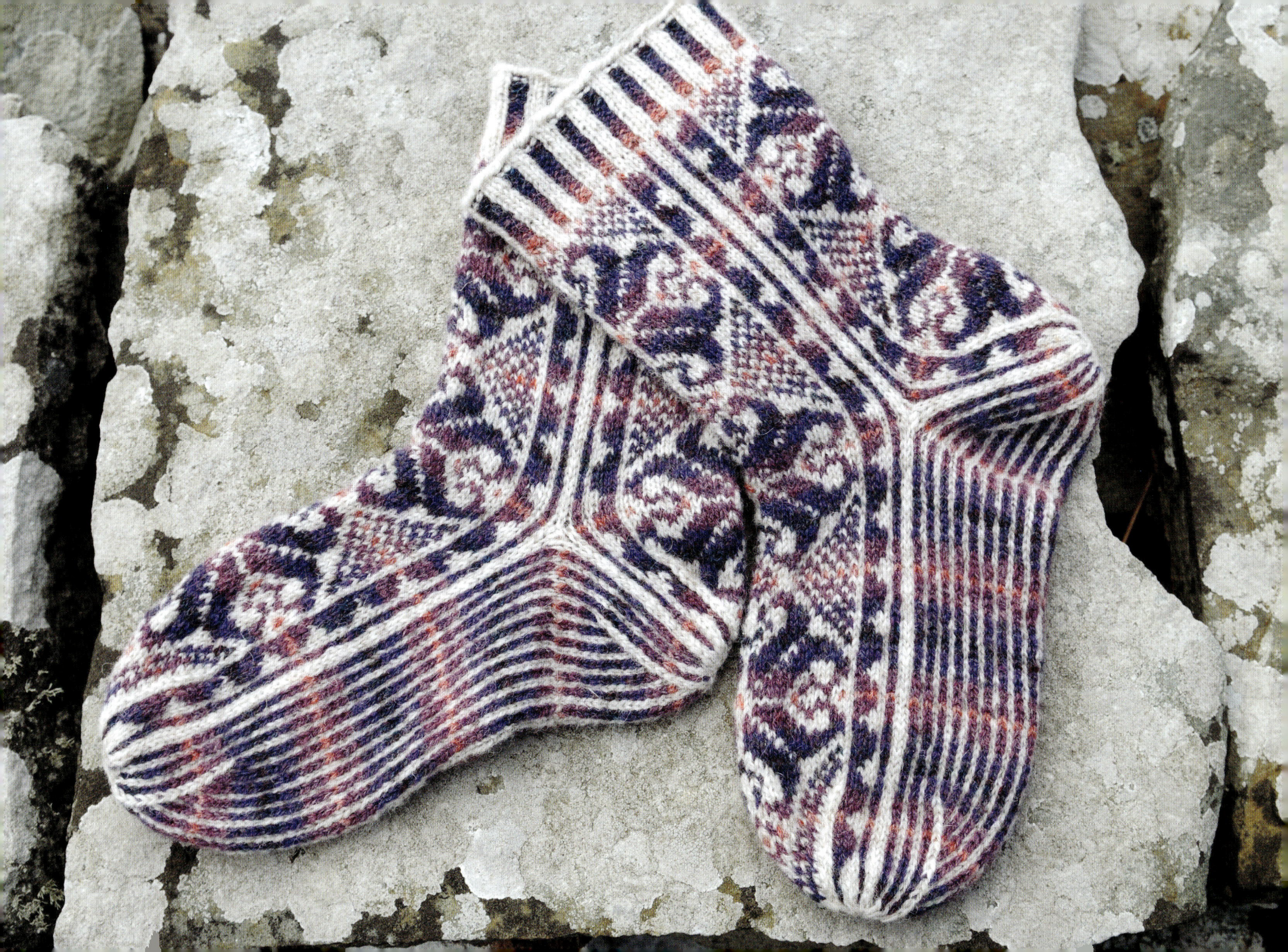

Toe

Next rnd (chart B row 88): Work 41 sts from chart B as set (decreasing 2 sts as indicated), pm, work 6 sts in stripe patt as set, using yarn A SSK, work in stripe patt as set to last 8 sts, using yarn A K2tog, work in stripe patt to end of round. 78 sts.

Next rnd: Work to marker in pattern from chart B, slm, work 6 sts in patt as set, using yarn A SSK, work in patt as set to last 8 sts, using yarn A K2tog, work in patt to end of round. 74 sts.

Continue decreasing on every round, as set by last round, until you have worked row 100 of chart B (11 more rounds). 30 sts.

Next rnd: Using yarn A only, *(SSK) 3 times, s2kpo, (K2tog) 3 times; rep from * once more. 14 sts.

Break yarn and thread through remaining stitches. Fasten off securely.

Heel

Carefully remove waste yarn at heel, and pick up the resulting 41 sts from above and below the opening. 82 sts.

Re-join yarns A and E (leaving tails of approx. 5cm/2in for weaving in later) at start of sole stitches, placing marker here for the start of the round.

Rnd 1: *K1A, K1E; rep from * 19 more times, K1A, pm, work 41 sts in patt from chart C row 1.

Last round sets stripe and chart C Fair Isle pattern. Use the same colours for the stripe pattern as you have been using in the charted pattern (so change from yarn E to yarn D when working next row of chart C).

Continue as set until row 7 of chart C has been completed.

Rnd 8: Work 6 sts in stripe patt as set, using yarn A SSK, work in stripe patt as set to last 8 sts before marker, using yarn A K2tog, work in stripe patt to marker, slm, work to end of round in pattern as shown on row 8 of chart C, decreasing sts as indicated. 78 sts.

Work as set by last round, using correct row of chart C, until row 20 is complete. 30 sts.

Rnd 21: Using yarn A only, *(SSK) 3 times, s2kpo, (K2tog) 3 times; rep from * once more. 14 sts.

Break yarn and thread through remaining stitches. Fasten off securely.

Finishing

Darn in all ends.

At the junction of the heel and sock leg there may be small holes. To close them, sew the tail ends of yarn around the back of the junction stitches in a circle and pull tight.

Chart Key

- Yarn A (2006); Knit
- Yarn A (2006); SSK
- Yarn A (2006); K2tog
- Yarn B (FC14); Knit
- Yarn B (FC14); Purl
- Yarn C (FC56); Knit
- Yarn C (FC56); Purl
- Yarn D (133); Knit
- Yarn D (133); Purl
- Yarn E (72); Knit
- Yarn E (72); Purl
- Pattern repeat

Chart A

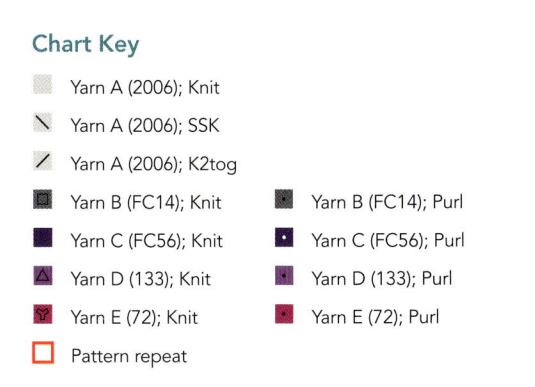

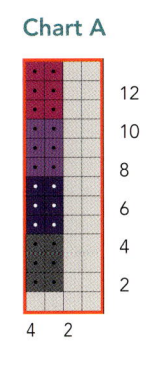

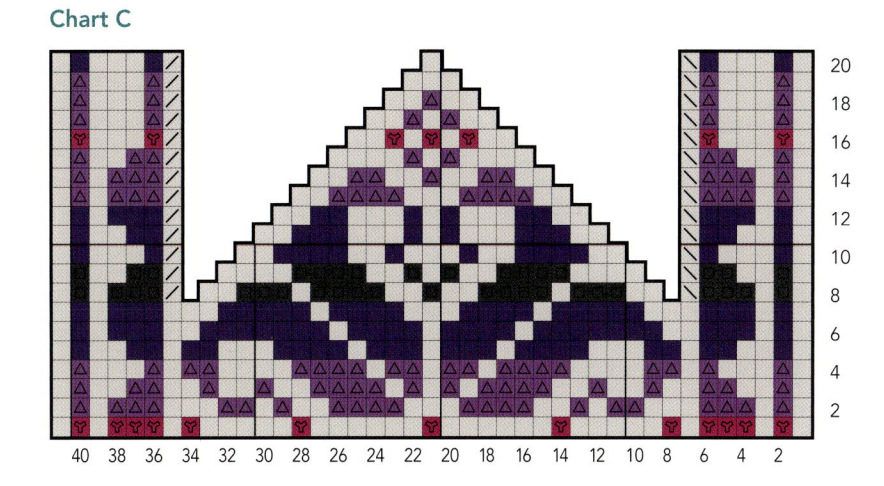

Chart C

Chart B

Muckleberry Gloves & Hat

designed by Mary Jane Mucklestone

Materials

Jamieson & Smith 2 Ply Jumper Weight – 100% Real Shetland Wool (115m/25g ball)

- Yarn A – Shade FC38: 1 x 25g ball
- Yarn B – Shade 5: 1 x 25g ball
- Yarn C – Shade 82: 1 x 25g ball
- Yarn D – Shade 134: 1 x 25g ball
- Yarn E – Shade FC12: 1 x 25g ball
- Yarn F – Shade 125: 1 x 25g balls

If both Gloves and Hat are made, two balls of yarn A will be required, but only 1 ball of each of the other shades.

3mm (UK 11/US 2–3) DPNs (for gloves only)

2.75mm (UK 12/US 2) circular needle, 40cm/16in long and DPNs (for hat only)

3.25mm (UK 10/US 3) circular needle, 40cm/16in long and DPNs (for hat only)

Stitch markers
Tapestry needle
25.5cm/10in diameter plate or cardboard disk for blocking tam

Sizing

Gloves: To fit adult hand circumference: 19–21.5cm/7.5–8.5in. Actual hand circumference above thumb, unstretched: 19cm/7.5in

Hat: To fit average adult head circumference: 50–55cm/19.5–20.5in. Actual circumference at brim 50cm/19.5in

Tension

Gloves: 32 sts and 32 rounds = 10cm/4in over Fair Isle pattern using 3mm needles
Hat: 30 sts and 32 rounds = 10cm/4in over Fair Isle pattern using 3.25mm needles

Abbreviations

See page 76.

To knit Muckleberry Gloves

Right glove

Using 3mm needles and yarn B, cast on 56 sts using the Estonian cast-on method (or alternative stretchy cast-on method). Join to work in the round, taking care not to twist the sts. Place marker for the start of the round.

Rnd 1: Using yarn B only *K1, P1; rep from * to end of round. Join in yarn A.

Rnd 2: *K1A, P1B; rep from * to end of round.

Last round sets two-colour rib. Work a further 8 rounds in two-colour rib as set.

Rnd 11: Using yarn B only, knit.

Rnds 12–22: Work from chart A (wrist), repeating the 14-stitch motif 4 times in each round. Join in new colours as required and use the Fair Isle technique. Cont to work from chart A, until row 11 of chart is complete.

Rnd 23: Using yarn B only, knit.

Rnds 24–32: As round 2.

**Rnd 33 (inc): Using yarn B only and picking up a strand of yarn B for the increases, K5, M1R, K6, M1R, K7, M1L, K6, M1L, K8, M1R, K5, M1R, K11, M1L, K5, M1L, K3. 64 sts.

Rnd 34 (start thumb gusset): Work 33 sts from row 1 of chart B (back of hand), pm, using yarn A M1R, K1B, using yarn A M1L, pm, *K1B, K1A; rep from * to end of round. 66 sts.

Rnd 35: Work 33 sts from row 2 of chart B, slm, K1B, K1A, K1B, slm, K2B, *K1A, K1B; rep from * to end of round (first st after marker is always in foreground colour, remaining sts are alternating to create speckled colour patt).

Rnd 36: Work from row 3 of chart B to marker, slm, using yarn B M1L, K1A, K1B, K1A, using yarn B M1R, slm, K1B, work in speckled colour patt as set to end of round. 68 sts.

Continue to work in patt from chart B on back of hand, and increase 2 sts in thumb gusset on next 7 alternate rounds as set, maintaining speckled colour patt on both thumb sts and on palm of hand, as well as column of foreground colour stitches at either end of thumb gusset. 82 sts.

Rnd 51: Work in patts as set without shaping (row 18 of chart B).

Rnd 52 (separate thumb): Work from row 19 of chart B to marker, slm, slip next 19 sts to waste yarn or a stitch holder, remove marker, using yarn B cast on 3 sts, continue in patt to end of round. 66 sts.

Rnd 53: Work from row 20 of chart B over 33 sts, work to end of round in speckled colour patt as set.

Work a further 4 rounds as set by last round, thus completing chart B.

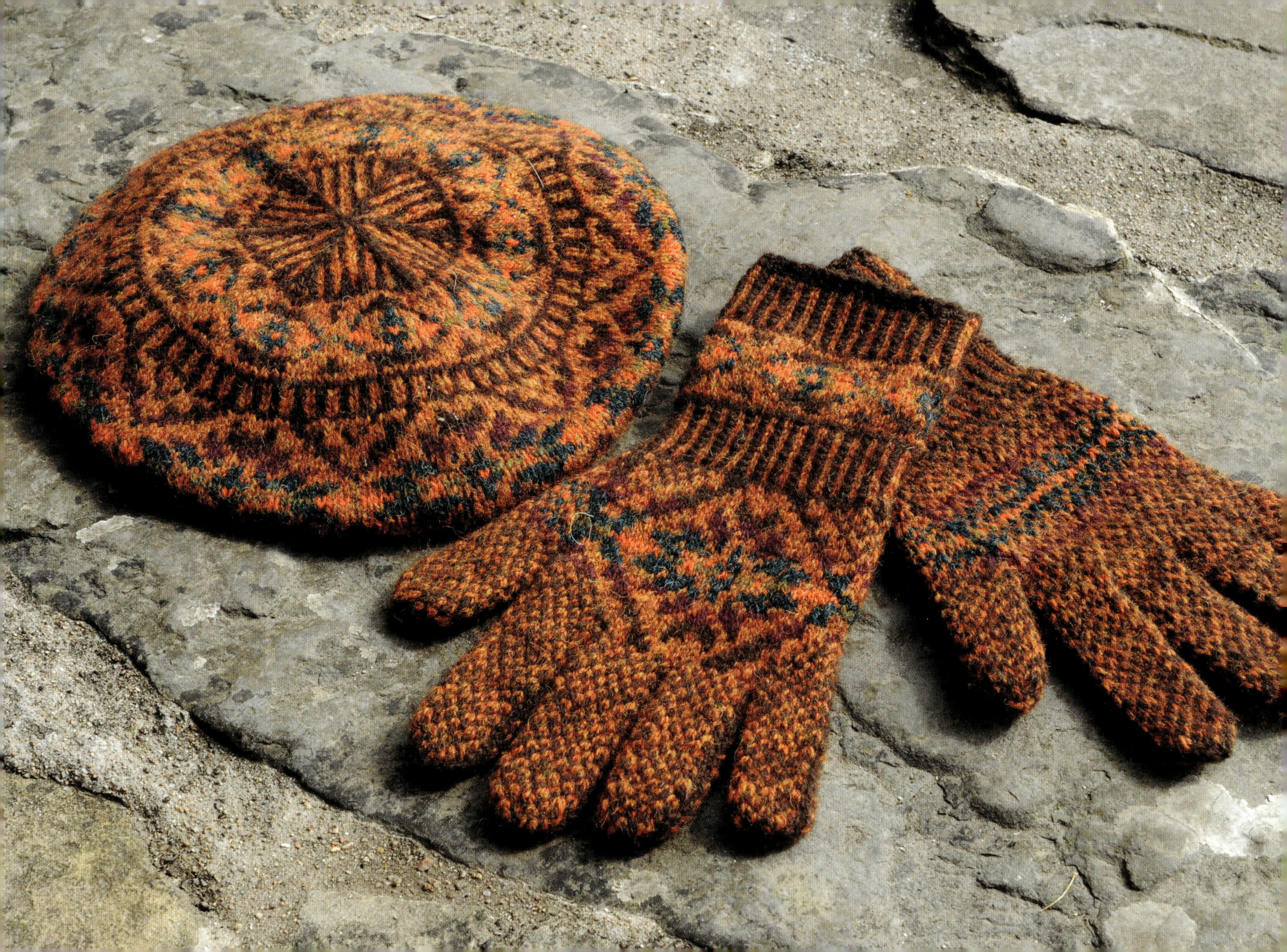

Little finger

†Next rnd: K1B, K7 in speckled colour patt (to match previous sts), place foll 50 sts on holder (for back hand and palm), using the backward loop method, cast on 3 sts in patt working last "seam" st in yarn B, K8 in speckled colour patt from palm. Place marker for start of round. 19 sts.

Next rnd: K1B, K9 in speckled colour patt, K1B, K8 in speckled colour patt.

Repeat last round until little finger measures 5cm/2in (or 6mm/0.25in less than desired length).

Next rnd (dec): *K1B, K2tog, knit to 2 sts before "seam" st, SSK, K1B; rep from * once more. 15 sts.

Repeat last round once more. 11 sts. Break yarn A, leaving 10cm/4in tail.

Using yarn B only, repeat decrease round once more. 7 sts. Break yarn, thread through remaining stitches and fasten off securely.

Ring finger

From holder, slip first and last 8 sts onto needles (34 sts rem on holder).

Next rnd: Re-join yarns A and B and working along cast-on edge of little finger, pick up and knit 1 stitch in patt, pick up and knit 1 stitch in yarn B for "seam" st and pick up and knit 1 stitch in patt, K8 sts from back of hand in pattern, use the backward loop method to cast on 3 sts in patt working centre "seam" st in yarn B, K8 in patt from palm, K1 further st in patt from those picked up at start of round. Place marker for start of round. 22 sts.

Next rnd: *K1B, K10 in speckled pattern; rep from * once more.

Repeat last round until little finger measures 7cm/2.75in (or 6mm/0.25in less than desired length).

Next rnd (dec): *K1B, K2tog, knit to 2 sts before "seam" st, SSK, K1B; rep from * once more. 18 sts.

Repeat last round 2 more times. 10 sts. Break yarn A, leaving 10cm/4in tail.

Using yarn B only, repeat decrease round once more. 6 sts. Break yarn, thread through remaining stitches and fasten off securely.

Middle finger

Work in the same manner as ring finger, but picking up sts along cast-on edge of ring finger, and working until finger measures 7.5cm/3in. There will be 18 sts remaining on holder.

Index finger

Return rem 18 sts to needles.

Next rnd: Working along cast-on edge of middle finger, pick up 1 stitch in patt, 1 stitch in yarn B for "seam" st, 1 stitch in patt, K18 in patt, K1 further st in patt from those picked up at start of round. Place marker for start of round. 21 sts.

Next rnd: K1B, patt to established "seam" st, K1B, patt to end.

Complete as for ring finger, noting that you will have 1 less stitch after each decrease round.

Thumb

Return 19 thumb sts to needles.

Next rnd: Using yarn B, pick up and knit 4 sts along cast-on edge between thumb and hand, alternating between yarns A & B, work in patt as set over 19 thumb sts. Place marker for start of round. 23 sts.

Next rnd: Work in alternating yarns A & B as set by previous round, to create speckled colour patt.

Repeat last round until thumb measures 5cm/2in (or 6mm/0.25in less than desired length).

Next rnd: Keeping patt correct, K3tog, (K2tog) 10 times. 11 sts.

Next rnd: (K2tog) 5 times, K1. 6 sts.

Break yarn, thread through remaining stitches and fasten off securely.

Glove/Hat Chart Key

- Yarn B (5); Knit
- Yarn A (FC38); Knit
- Yarn C (82); Knit
- Yarn F (125); Knit
- Yarn E (FC12); Knit
- Yarn D (134); Knit
- Yarn B (5); K2tog
- Yarn B (5); s2kpo

Chart A (Glove)

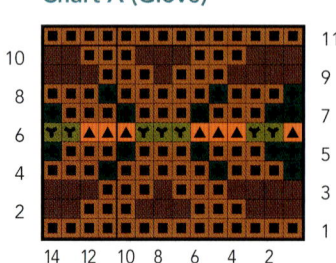

Chart B (Glove)

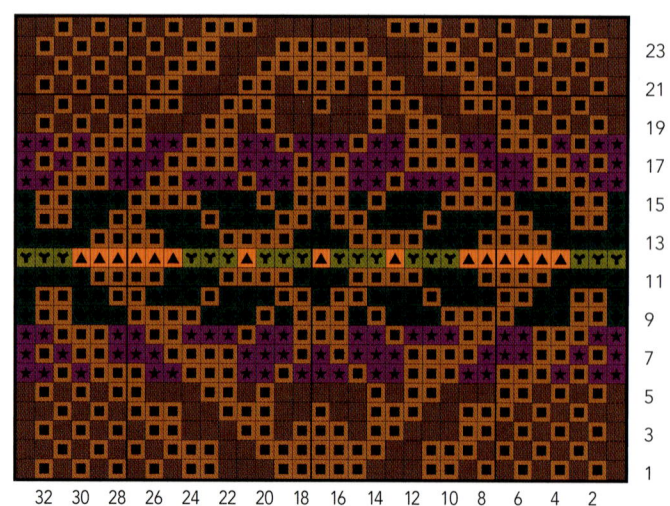

Chart C (Hat)

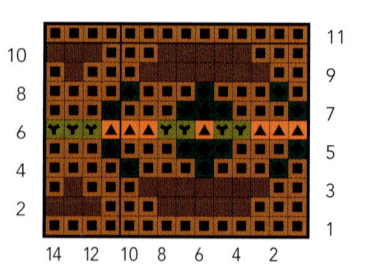

Left glove

Make as for Right Glove to **.

Rnd 33 (inc): Using yarn B only and picking up a strand of yarn B for the increases, K4, M1R, K5, M1R, K11, M1L, K5, M1L, K8, M1R, K6, M1R, K7, M1L, K6, M1L, K4. 64 sts.

Rnd 34 (start thumb gusset): Work 33 sts from row 1 of chart B (back of hand), pm, *K1B, K1A; rep from * to last 3 sts, K2B, pm (for thumb), using yarn A M1R, K1B, using yarn A M1L. 66 sts.

Rnd 35: Work 33 sts from row 2 of chart B, slm, *K1A, K1B; rep from * to marker, slm, K1B, K1A, K1B (last st before thumb marker is always in foreground colour, remaining sts are alternating to create speckled colour patt).

Rnd 36: Work from row 3 chart B to marker, slm, work in speckled colour patt to last st before next marker, K1B, slm, using yarn B M1L, K1A, K1B, K1A, using yarn B M1R. 68 sts.

Continue to work in patt from chart B on back of hand, and increase 2 sts in thumb gusset on next 7 alternate rounds as set, maintaining speckled colour patt on both thumb sts and on palm of hand, as well as column of foreground colour stitches at either end of thumb gusset. 82 sts.

Rnd 51: Work in patts as set without shaping (row 18 of chart B).

Rnd 52 (separate thumb): Work from row 19 of chart B to marker, slm, work in speckled pattern to last st before marker, K1B, remove marker, slip next 19 sts to waste yarn or a stitch holder, using yarn B cast on 3 sts. 66 sts.

Rnd 53: Work from row 20 of chart B over 33 sts, work to end of round in speckled colour patt as set.

Work a further 4 rounds as set by last round, thus completing chart B.

Next rnd (partial): Remove start of round marker, work in speckled colour patt over 32 sts (as set by edges of chart D pattern), place new marker for start of round.

Complete left glove as right glove from †.

Chart D (Hat)

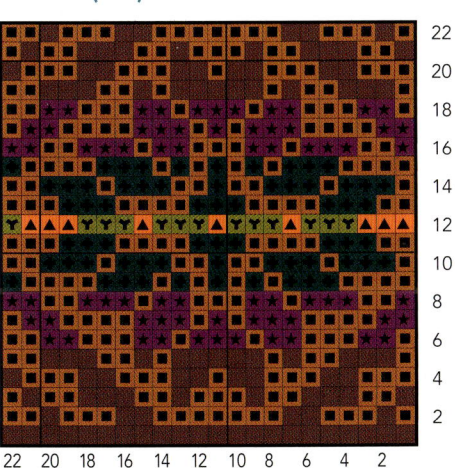

Chart E (Hat)

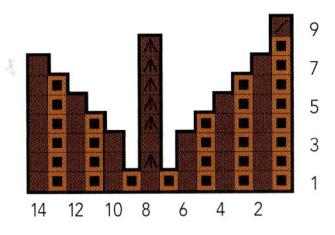

Finishing

Wash (see page 79) and lay flat to dry, smoothing stitches with your fingers to even colourwork. Darn in loose ends, carefully closing up any gaps between fingers and at the base of thumb.

To knit Muckleberry Hat

Brim

Using 2.75mm needles and yarn B, cast on 140 sts. Join to work in the round, taking care not to twist sts. Place marker for start of the round.

Next rnd: *K1A, P1B; rep from * to end.

Last round sets two colour rib pattern. Repeat last round until piece measures 4cm/1.5in.

Next rnd (inc): Using yarn B *K5, M1; rep from * 27 more times. 168 sts.

Change to 3.25mm needles.

Work from chart C, repeating the 14-stitch motif 12 times in each round. Join in new colours as required and use the Fair Isle technique.

Cont to work from chart C, until row 11 of chart is complete.

Rnd 12 (inc): Using yarn B *K21, M1; rep from * 7 more times. 176 sts.

Next rnd: *K1A, K1B; rep from * to end of round.

Repeat last round 2 more times.

Work rounds 1–22 of chart D, repeating the 22-stitch motif 8 times in each round.

Next rnd (dec): Using yarn B *K2, K2tog; rep from * 43 more times. 132 sts.

Next rnd: *K1A, K1B; rep from * to end of round.

Repeat last round 2 more times.

Next rnd (dec): Using yarn B *K20, K2tog; rep from * 5 more times. 126 sts.

Work rounds 1–11 of chart C, repeating 14-stitch motif 9 times in each round.

Next rnd (dec): Using yarn B *K1, K2tog; rep from * to end of round. 84 sts.

Top

Work rounds 1–9 of chart E, repeating the motif 6 times in each round, and decreasing as indicated. 6 sts.

Break yarn, thread through remaining stitches and fasten off securely.

Finishing

Darn in loose ends. Wash (see page 79) and block to finished measurement by stretching over a cardboard disk or dinner plate. The soft "fold" line should be at approximately round 12 of chart B.

Caavie Gansey

designed by Candace Eisner Strick

Materials

Jamieson & Smith 2 Ply Jumper Weight – 100% Real Shetland Wool
(118m/25g balls)

- Yarn A – Shade 202: 9 (10) x 25g balls
- Yarn B – Shade 36: 5 (6) x 25g balls
- Yarn C – Shade FC47: 2 (3) x 25g balls
- Yarn D – Shade 366: 2 (3) x 25g balls
- Yarn E – Shade 133: 2 (3) x 25g balls
- Yarn F – Shade 134: 1 (1) x 25g ball

2.5mm (UK 13–12/US 1–2) circular needles or long DPNs
3mm (UK 11/US 2–3) circular needles or long DPNs

Tapestry needle
Stitch markers
Sharp scissors

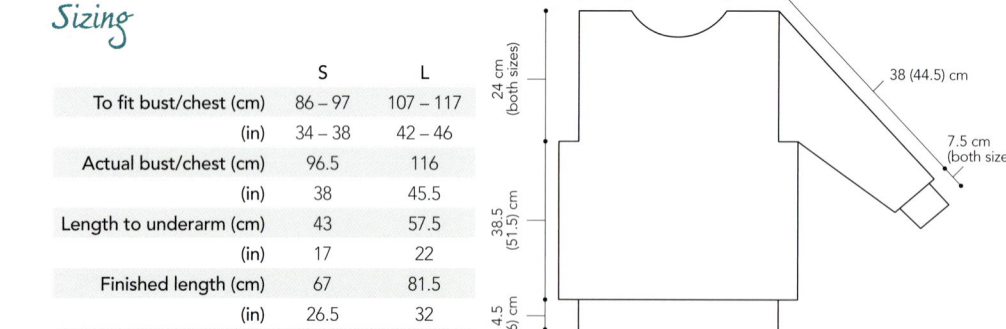

Sizing

	S	L
To fit bust/chest (cm)	86 – 97	107 – 117
(in)	34 – 38	42 – 46
Actual bust/chest (cm)	96.5	116
(in)	38	45.5
Length to underarm (cm)	43	57.5
(in)	17	22
Finished length (cm)	67	81.5
(in)	26.5	32
Sleeve* (cm)	45.5	52
(in)	18	20.5

Size shown in photograph is S (96.5cm/38in bust/chest).

*Sleeve is measured from shoulder.

Tension

29 sts and 31 rows = 10cm/4in over Fair Isle patt using 3mm needles

Chart notes

As this garment is knitted in the round, all chart rows are read from right to left.

Abbreviations

See page 76.

Pattern notes

The body of the sweater is worked in the round. At the armholes, you will cast on steek stitches. These 10 extra stitches form a bridge where the armhole openings will be, and allow work to continue in the round. Later on, these steek stitches will be cut up the middle to form the armhole opening, trimmed, and hemmed down. The sleeve stitches will be picked up around this opening, and the sleeves worked down to the cuff.

To knit Caavie Gansey

Body

With 2.5mm needle and yarn B, cast on 280 (336) sts. Join to work in the round, taking care not to twist sts and place a marker for the start of the round.

Rnds 1 and 2: Purl.

Rnds 3 and 4: Knit.

Repeat last 4 rounds 6 (7) more times.

Change to 3mm needles.

Next rnd: Work from chart A, row 1, working the 28-st repeat indicated for your size 10 (12) times.

Cont to work from chart A as set, until the 40 rows of chart A have been worked 2 (3) times in total.

Work rows 1–39 from chart A once more.

Next rnd: Work from chart A, row 40, patt 140 (168) sts, pm, work in patt to end of round. The two markers now divide your work into front and back.

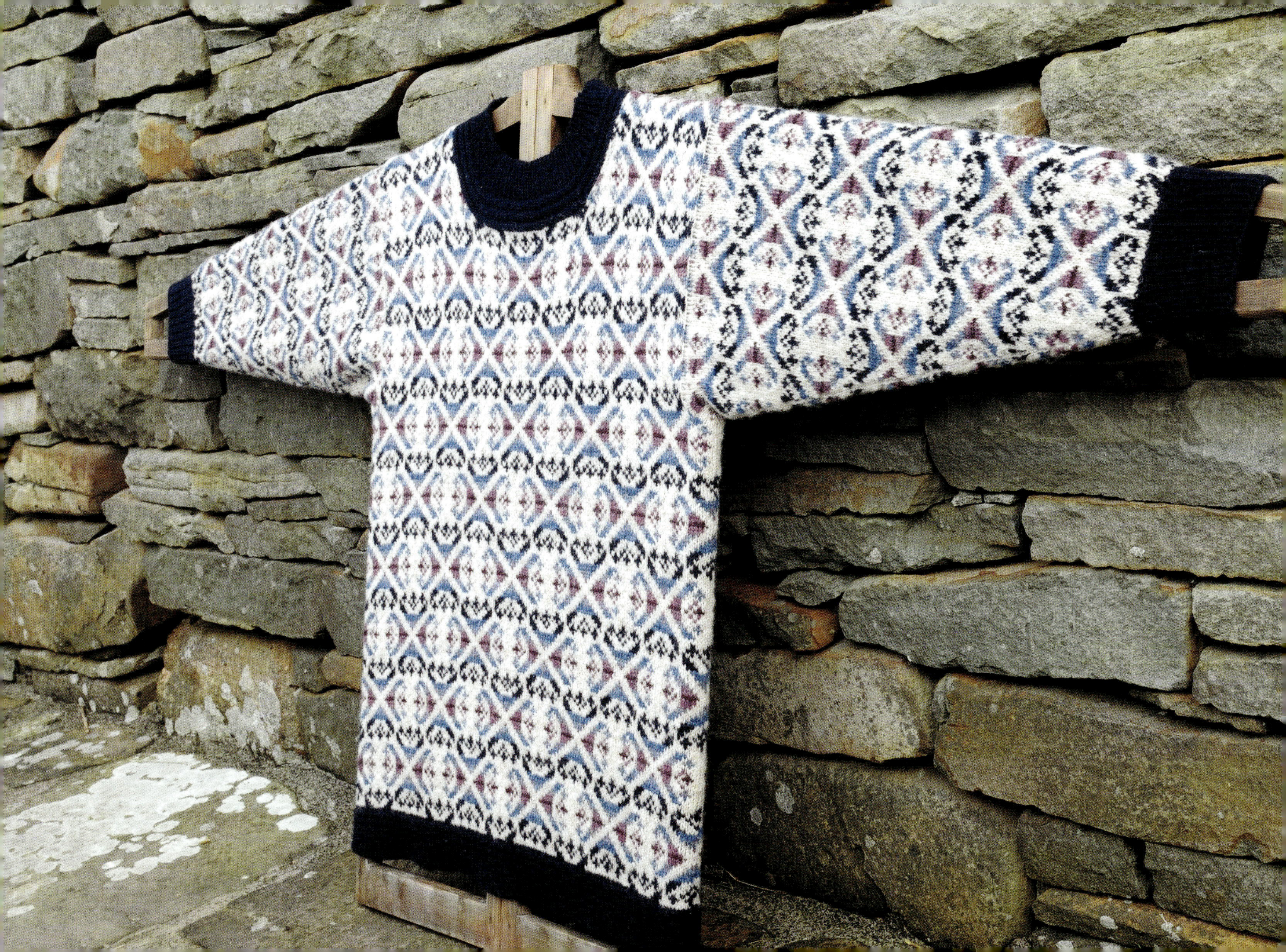

Divide for armholes and begin steeks
Front and back are worked alike to neck shaping.

Next rnd: *Keeping pattern correct, work from chart A, row 1 to 6 sts before next marker, place the next 13 sts on a spare needle or stitch holder, pm, cast on 10 steek sts using alternating colours, pm; rep from * once more. 274 (330) sts, including 20 steek sts.

You will now be working on 127 (155) sts each for the front and the back.

Next rnd: *Work from chart B, starting at row 2 beginning at the line indicated for your size, work to the end of the repeat section for your size, then work the 28 st repeat as normal to marker, slm, knit 10 steek sts in alternating colours, slm, work from chart B row 2 as before to marker, slm, knit 5 steek sts in alternating colours, pm (this is new start of round marker).

All rounds now begin and end at the new marker position in the centre of the steek, and this is where all new colours will be joined in. Ends do not need to be worked in anymore, since the steek will be cut and the ends trimmed away.

Next rnd: *Knit 5 steek sts in alternating colours (reversing order from last round), slm, work from chart B row 3 to next marker, slm, knit 5 steek sts in alternating colours (reversing order from last round); rep from * once more.

This round sets patt for steek sts and chart B. Cont to work from chart B until row 40 is complete, then work rows 1–7 once more.

Shape neck
Rnd 1: K5 steek sts as set, slm, following chart C row 1, work 44 (58) sts, put middle 39 sts on a holder for the front neck, pm, cast on 10 sts for front neck steek using alternating colours, pm, work remaining 44 (58) sts of front from chart C, then complete the round as previously set. This front steek is worked exactly the same as the armhole steeks. 245 (301) sts, including 30 steek sts.

Rnds 2–6 (front neck decs): K5 steek sts as set, slm, work from chart C to 2 sts before next marker, K2tog, slm, K10 front neck steek sts, slm, SSK, work from chart C to next marker, slm, K10 armhole steek sts, slm, work from chart C to next marker, slm, K5 armhole steek sts to complete round.

Rnd 7: Keeping pattern correct, work without shaping.

Rnd 8 (front neck dec): As round 2.

Rnds 9 and 10: As round 7.

Repeat last 3 rounds twice more. 229 (285) sts, including 30 steek sts.

Rnd 17 (front neck dec): As round 2. 227 (283) sts, including 30 steek sts.

Rnd 18: As round 7.

Rnd 19: K5 steek sts as set, slm, work from chart C to next marker, slm, K10 front neck steek sts, slm, work from chart C to next marker, slm, K10 armhole steek sts, work 40 (54) sts from chart C, place next 47 sts on a holder for back neck, pm, cast on 10 back neck steek sts using alternating colours, pm, work rem 40 (54) sts from chart C, slm, K5 armhole steek sts. 190 (246) sts, including 40 steek sts.

Rnd 20 (front neck dec): As round 2. 188 (244) sts, including 40 steek sts.

Rnds 21 and 22 (back neck decs): K5 steek sts, slm, work from chart C to next marker, slm, K10 front neck steek sts, slm, work from chart C to next marker, slm, K10 armhole steek sts, slm, work from chart C to 2 sts before next marker, K2tog, slm, K10 back neck steek sts, slm, SSK, work from chart C to next marker, slm, K5 steek sts. 184 (240) sts, including 40 steek sts.

Rnd 23 (front & back neck decs): Dec 1 st at each side of both front and back neck steeks as set. 180 (236) sts, including 40 steek sts.

Rnds 24 & 25 (back neck decs): As round 21. 176 (232) sts, including 40 steek sts.

Rnd 26 (end front & back neck dec): Cast off 5 armhole steek sts, work front as set to marker, rm, cast off 10 front neck steek sts, rm, work front as set to marker, rm, cast off 10 armhole steek sts, rm, work to 2 sts before marker, K2tog, slm, K10 back neck steek sts, slm, SSK, work to marker, rm, cast off remaining 5 steek sts of armhole. Place 33 (47) sts on each side for front shoulders on holders.

Rnd 27: Re-join yarn at right armhole, work to 2 sts before steek marker, K2tog, cast off 9 steek sts, K2tog, cast off last steek st over this K2tog stitch, work remaining sts. Place 33 (47) sts on holders for back shoulders.

Cutting the steeks
Using the zigzag stitch on a sewing machine, or backstitching by hand, sew through all cast-on and cast-off edges of all steeks. Using a sharp pair of scissors, cut up the middle of the steeks between sts 5 and 6. Trim away the ends left from changing colours.

Turn back the 5 steek sts, hemming them down by hand using an overcast stitch. Be careful that your stitching does not show through on the right side. When you have finished, work back over the stitches in the opposite direction, forming Xs.

Steam gently.

Join shoulders
Return left front and back shoulder stitches to needles. Turn the work inside out and use a third needle to knit together the first stitch from each needle. *Knit together the next stitch from each needle. You will now have 2 sts on right-hand needle, cast off 1 st in the normal way. Rep from * until all of the left shoulder stitches have been cast off.

Repeat for right shoulder stitches.

Neckband
Note: When picking up sts around openings that have been steeked, use the st directly adjacent to the last steek st. Insert the needle through both loops of the st, draw yarn through, and knit.

With RS facing, and starting at the left shoulder seam, using 2.5mm needle and yarn B, pick up and knit 28 sts down the left front, knit 39 sts from front neck holder, pick up and knit 28 sts up right front neck to shoulder seam, pick up and knit 10 sts down the right back, knit the 47 sts from the back neck holder, pick up and knit 10 sts up left back. 162 sts.

Rnds 1 and 2: Purl.

Rnds 3 and 4: Knit.

Work these 4 rounds once more, and then work rounds 1–3 again.

Rnd 12: K7, K2tog, *K5, K2tog; rep from * 20 more times, K6. 140 sts.

Rnd 13: *K1, P1; rep from * to end of round.

Last round sets rib. Work until rib meas 3.75cm/1.5in. Cast off in rib.

Sleeves

With RS facing, and using 3mm needles and yarn A, knit last 6 sts from underarm stitch holder, pick up and knit 75 sts to shoulder seam, pick up and knit another 75 sts to underarm, knit 6 sts from holder, pm, knit last stitch from holder, pm. 163 sts.

Rnd 1: Starting at row 32 on the fourth st from the right-hand side of chart D, knit to 28th stitch of chart (end of marked repeat) and then work the full 28-stitch repeat 4 times, then work first 25 sts of chart again, slm, K1 in yarn A, slm.

Rnd 2: As round 1 but working from row 33 of chart D.

Rnd 3: K2tog using yarn F (this is 5th st from right-hand side of chart D row 34), work in patt from 6th stitch to 28th stitch on chart (end of marked rep) and then work the 28-stitch repeat 4 times, work first 23 sts of chart again, SSK using yarn F, slm, K1 in yarn A, slm. 161 sts.

Working decreases as set by last round (keeping yarn used for dec as set by chart pattern and always working underarm stitch in yarn A), continue to decrease 1 st at each end of next 36 (40) third rounds. 89 (81) sts.

The lines numbered 1 to 5 on the chart show where to start the pattern on each round, if you follow them in order.

Change to double-pointed needles when necessary.

Work in pattern without further shaping for a further 5 (13) rounds. Round 27 (7) is complete.

Change to 2.5mm needles and yarn B only.

Small size only

Next rnd: *(K2tog) 5 times, K1; rep from * 6 more times, (K2tog) 6 times. 48 sts.

Large size only

Next rnd: K2tog, K1; rep from * to end of round. 54 sts.

Both sizes

Next rnd: *K1, P1; rep from * to end of round.

Last round sets rib. Work until rib measures 7.5cm/3in.

Cast off in rib.

Finishing

Darn in all ends. Wash (see page 79)

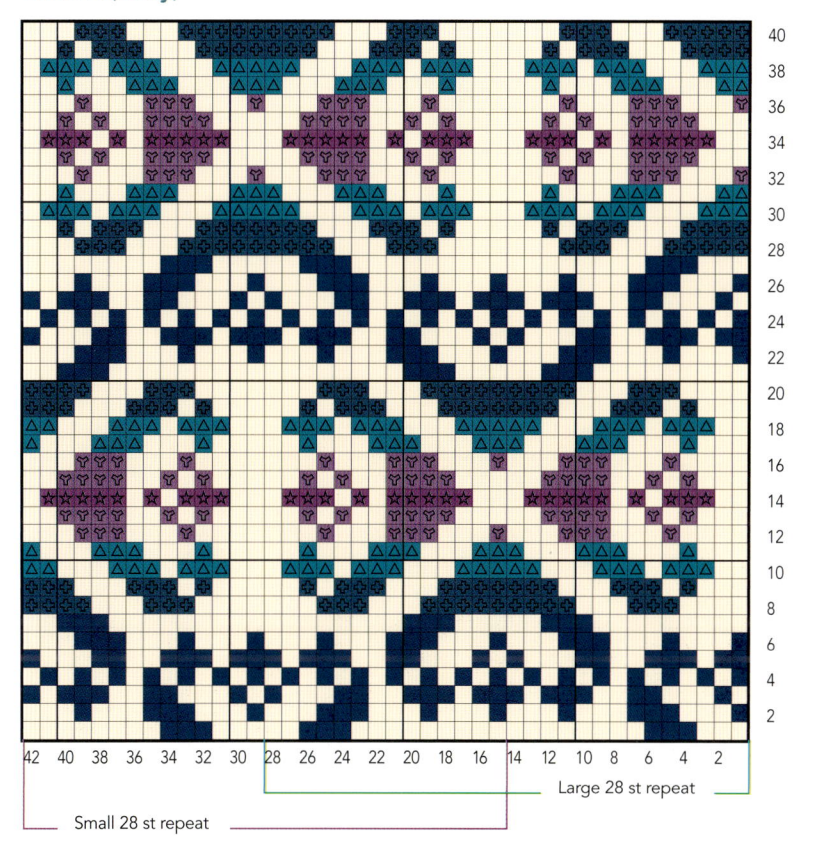

Chart Key

- Yarn A (202); Knit
- Yarn B (36); Knit
- Yarn C (FC47); Knit
- Yarn D (366); Knit
- Yarn E (133); Knit
- Yarn F (134); Knit

Chart A (Body)

Chart Key

- Yarn A (202); Knit
- Yarn B (36); Knit
- Yarn C (FC47); Knit
- Yarn D (366); Knit
- Yarn E (133); Knit
- Yarn F (134); Knit

Tinted area shows previous column for reference only. Do not knit.

Chart B (Armholes)

Large 28 st repeat

Small 28 st repeat

Small, start armhole

Large, start armhole

Chart C (Neck)

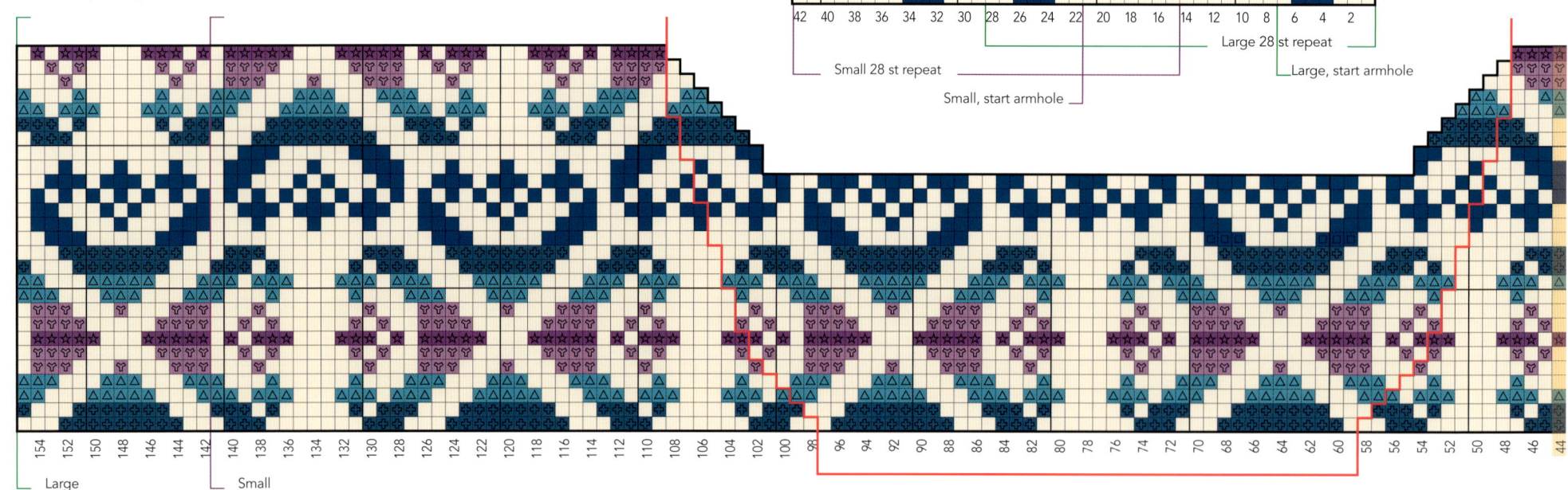

Large

Small

Chart D (Sleeves)

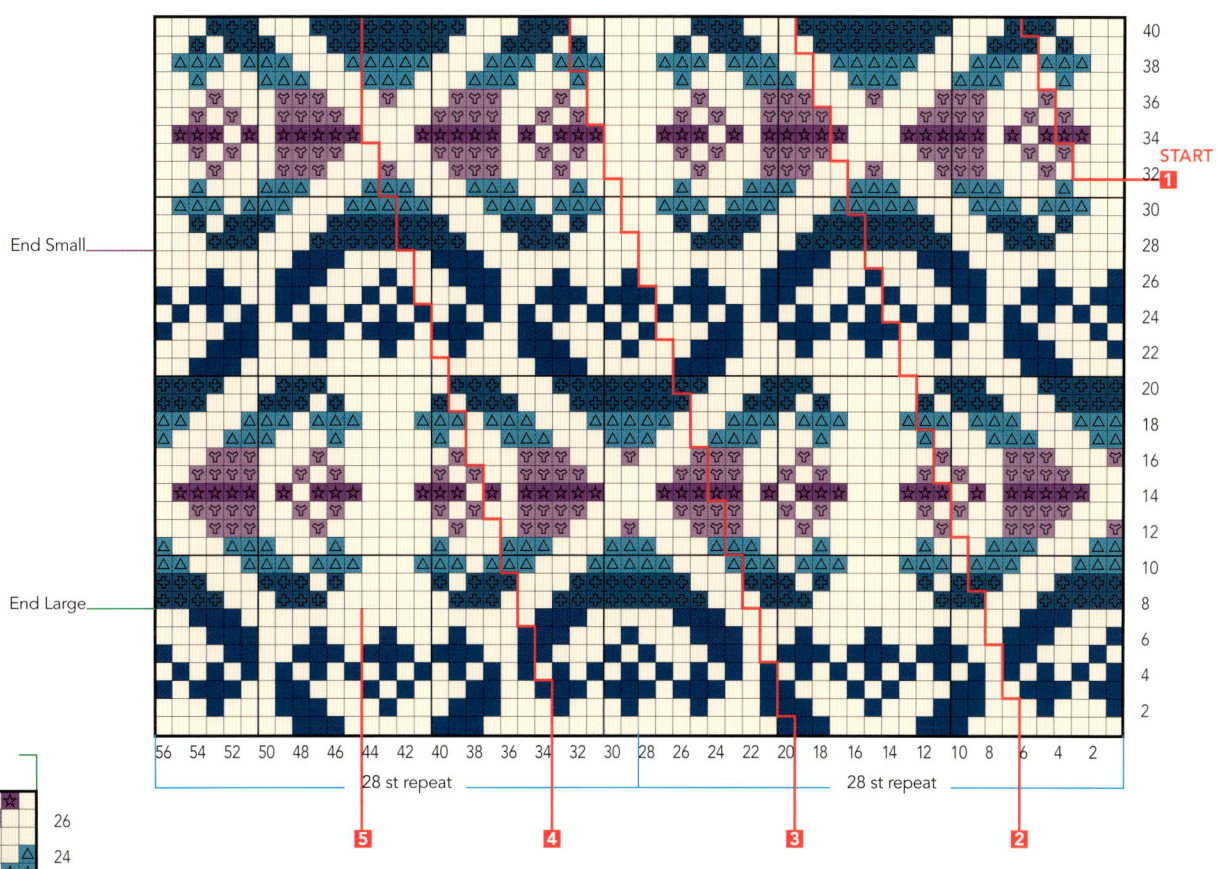

Chart C (Neck) continued

59

Madeira Lace Shawl

designed by Joyce Ward

Materials

Jamieson & Smith Shetland Supreme 2 Ply Lace Weight – 100% Real Shetland Wool (360m/25g balls)

- Shade Moorit: 4 x 25g balls

3.5mm (UK 10–9/US 4) needles

Tapestry needle

Sizing

One size only (measured relaxed after blocking).

Top to bottom: 95cm/38in
Along top edge: 190cm/76in

Tension

Measured relaxed after blocking

20 sts = 12cm/4.75in over lace patt using 3.5mm needles

20 rows = 7cm/2.75in over lace patt using 3.5mm needles

Abbreviations

See page 76.

Chart notes

All RS rows are read from right to left and all WS rows are read from left to right.

Pattern notes

This shawl is worked on a garter stitch background, so WS rows are worked with knit stitches.

Be sure to keep the stitch markers in the correct places – it is easy for them to slip under the yarn over stitches. In the main part of the shawl, the number of body stitches between the first and last (edging) markers increases by 4 stitches on every RS row. The number of edging stitches at each end (outside of the first and last markers) increases by 1 stitch on each RS row 5 times, and then decreases again by casting off 5 sts every 10 rows.

To knit Madeira Lace Shawl

Shawl

Cast on 29 sts.

Row 1 (RS, also shown on chart A): K2, yo, K2tog, yo, K1, K2tog, yo, K2, pm, yo, K5, yo, pm, K1, pm, yo, K5, yo, pm, K2, yo, Sl 1, K1, psso, K1, yo, Sl 1, K1, psso, yo, K2. 35 sts.

Row 2 (WS, also shown on chart A): K7, yo, K2tog, K1, slm, K7, slm, K1, slm, K7, slm, K1, Sl 1, K1, psso, yo, K7.

Cont to work from chart A until row 60 is complete. 154 sts.

Begin working main section as follows:

Row 61 (RS, also shown on charts): Work edging following row 1 chart C to first marker, slm, work from row 61 chart B, repeating the marked section twice on the first half of the row, and repeating the marked section twice on the second half of the row, slm, work edging sts following row 1 chart D to end. 155 sts.

Cont to work from charts as set, repeating 10 rows of edging charts as needed, until row 100 of chart B is complete. 234 sts.

Now repeat rows 61 to 100 of chart B, this time repeating the marked sections 4 times in each half of the rows. 314 sts.

Finally, repeat rows 61 to 100 once more, this time repeating the marked sections 6 times in each half of the rows. 394 sts.

Top Edging

You will now work back and forth over the edging stitches at the start of the RS row. As you work from chart E, at the end of each RS row you will knit together one of the edging stitches with one of the live stitches from the body of the shawl. In this way you will "cast off" all of the main body stitches of the shawl. For each 10 rows that you work, you will use up 5 of the body stitches of the shawl.

Following chart E, work and attach edging to the shawl, repeating rows 1 to 10 until 73 repeats have been completed.

Now work rows 11 to 20 from chart E.

Cast off 5 sts at the beg of the next row, work to end of edging row. Graft the remaining sts to edging sts at left side of shawl. Sew cast-on edge together, so that there is an unbroken strip of edging around the entire shawl.

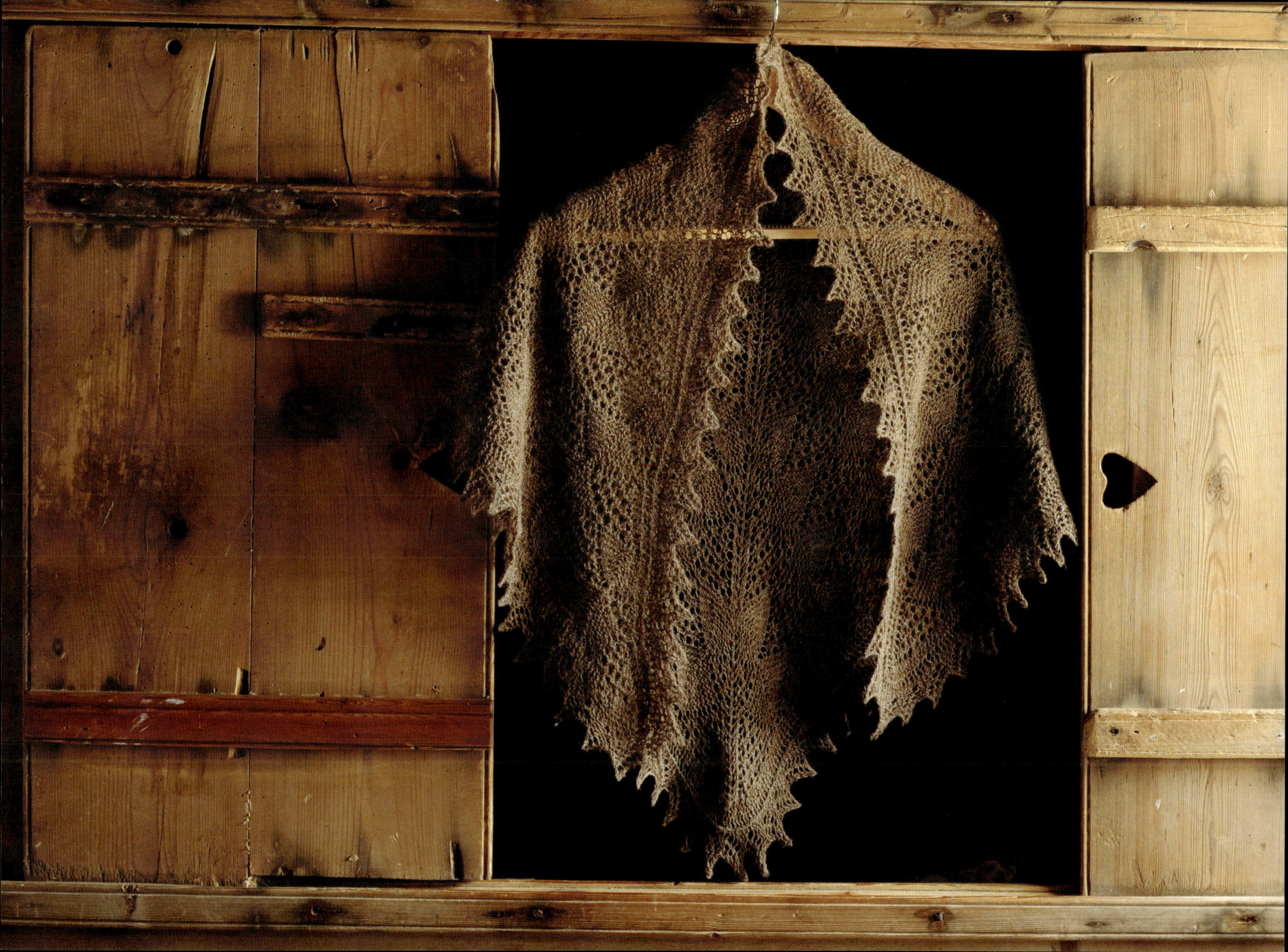

Finishing

Darn in all ends, but do not trim.

Wash (see page 79). Pin out to measurements (approx. 95cm/38in from top to bottom and 190cm/76in along the top edge) on a clean sheet on the floor or a mattress, and allow to dry fully.

Unpin and trim any ends.

Chart Key

- ☐ Knit on RS, Purl on WS
- ▨ Purl on RS, Knit on WS
- O Yarnover
- ╱ K2tog on RS, P2tog on WS
- ╲ Sl 1, K1, psso on RS, P2tog tbl on WS
- ╱ P2tog on RS, K2tog on WS
- ╲ P2tog tbl on RS, Sl 1, K1, psso on WS
- ⋏ Sl 1, K2tog, psso
- ⌒ Cast off knitwise on RS and purlwise on WS
- ⌒ Cast off purlwise on RS and knitwise on WS
- ● K2togE
- ▢ Pattern repeat
- ▦ Tinted area shows previous column for reference only. Do not knit.

Chart A

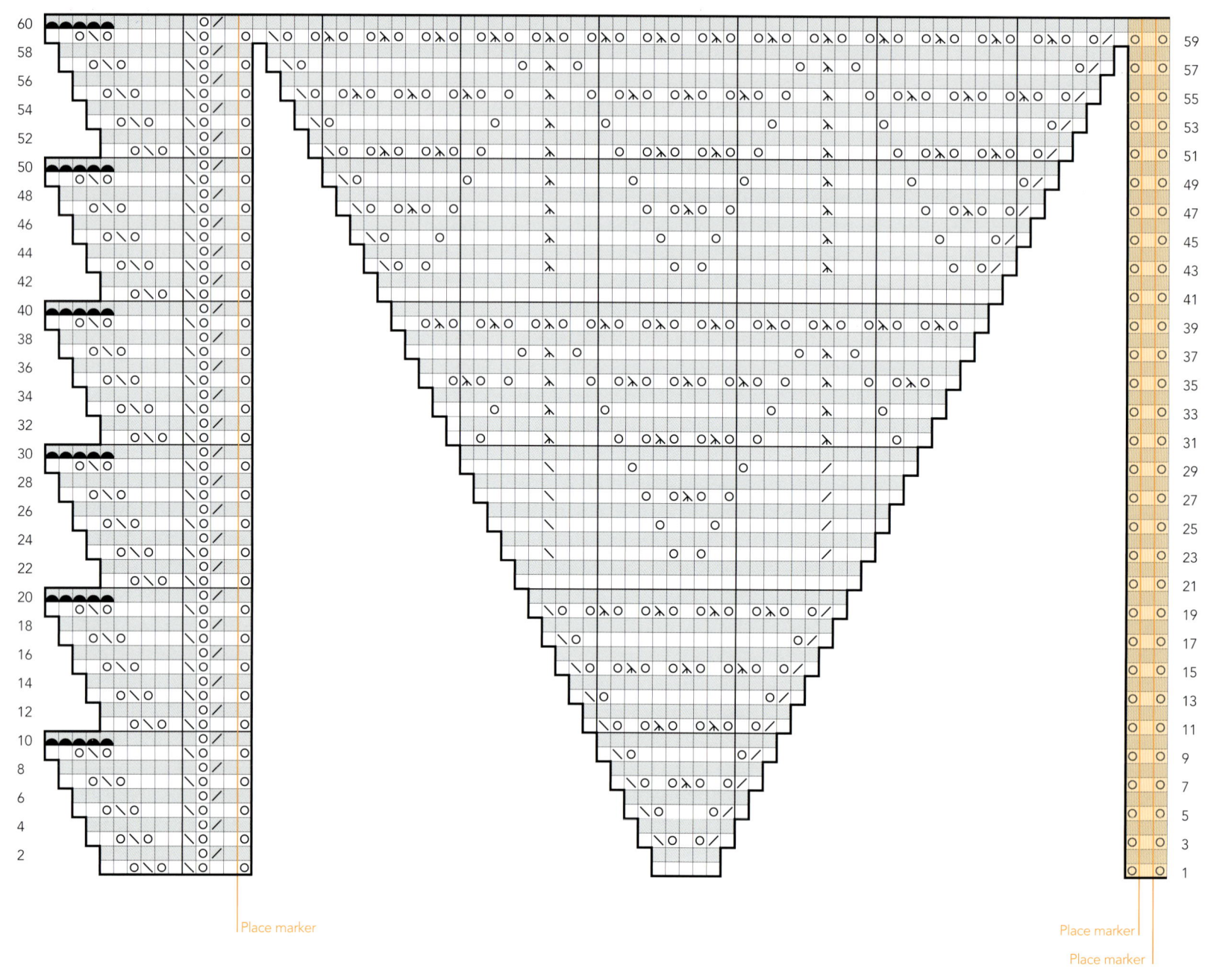

Chart A continued

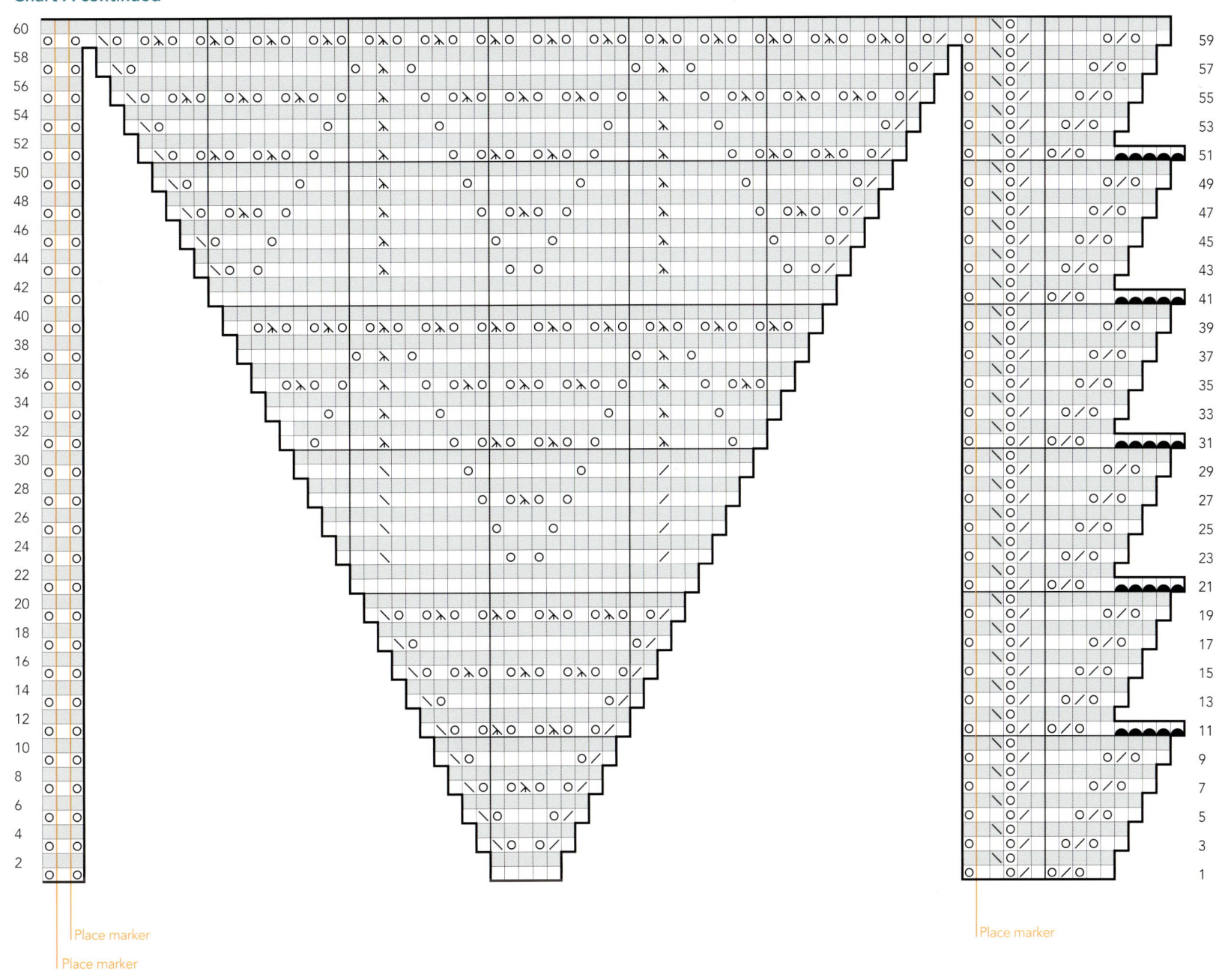

Chart B

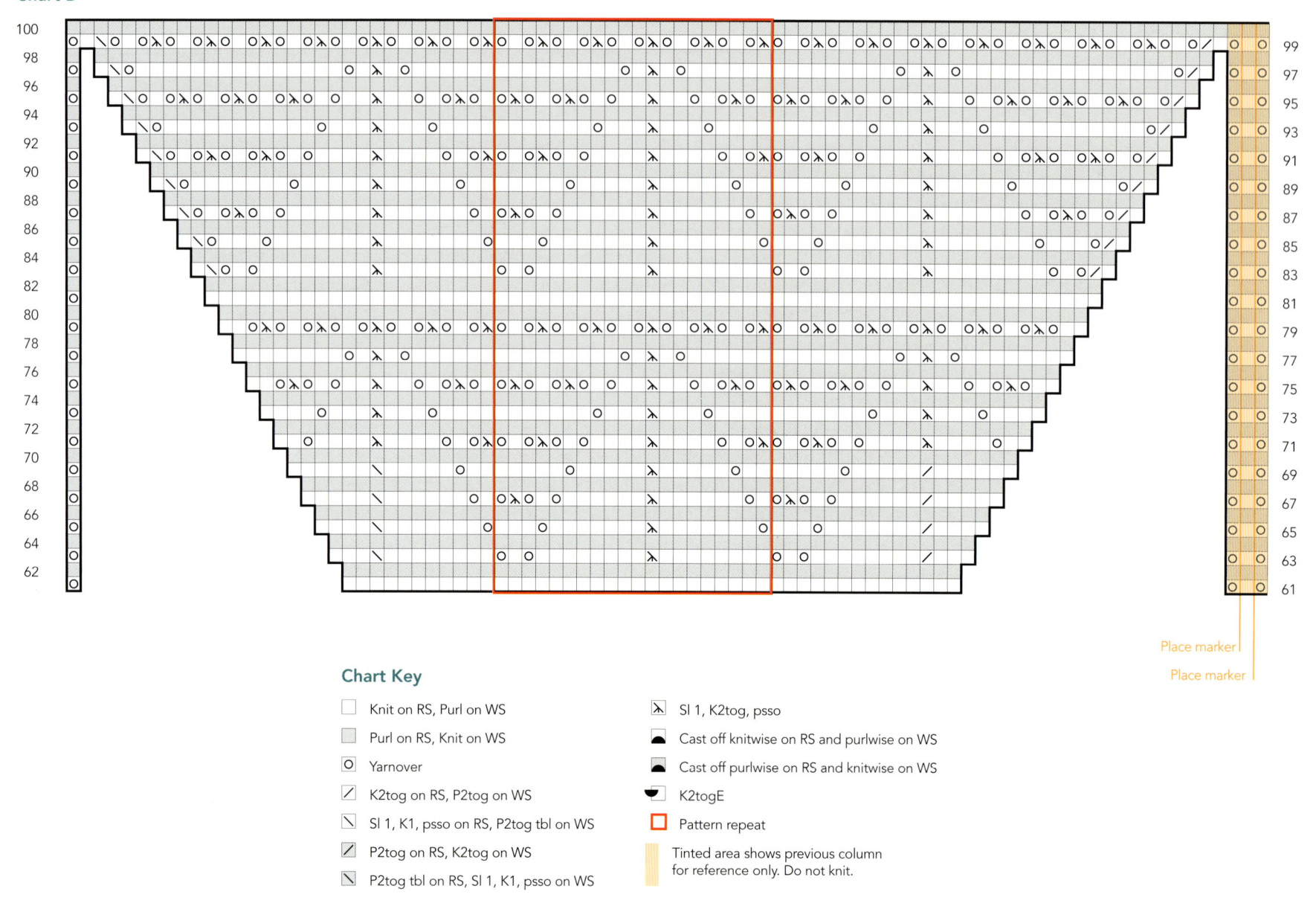

Chart Key

- ☐ Knit on RS, Purl on WS
- ▦ Purl on RS, Knit on WS
- ○ Yarnover
- ╱ K2tog on RS, P2tog on WS
- ╲ Sl 1, K1, psso on RS, P2tog tbl on WS
- ╱ P2tog on RS, K2tog on WS
- ╲ P2tog tbl on RS, Sl 1, K1, psso on WS
- ⋏ Sl 1, K2tog, psso
- ⬛ Cast off knitwise on RS and purlwise on WS
- ⬛ Cast off purlwise on RS and knitwise on WS
- ▼ K2togE
- ▯ Pattern repeat
- ▮ Tinted area shows previous column for reference only. Do not knit.

Chart B continued

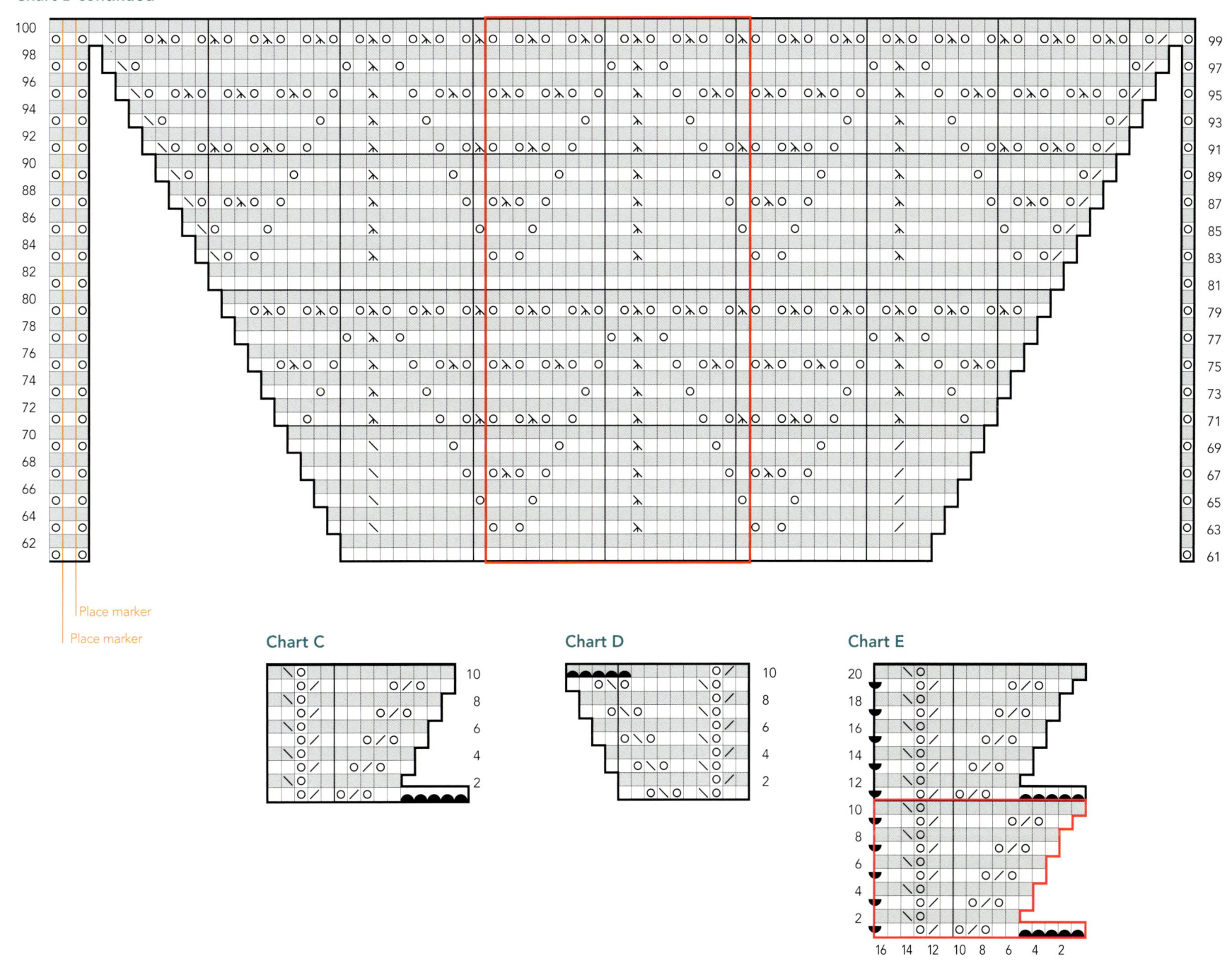

Chart C

Chart D

Chart E

Buttoned Hat
designed by Woolly Wormhead

Materials

Jamieson & Smith Shetland Aran – 100% Real Shetland Wool (90m/50g balls)

- Shade BSS9: 1 (2, 2) x 50g balls

4.5mm (UK 7/US 7) knitting needles
4.5mm (UK 7/US 7) DPNs (or your preferred needles for small diameter knitting in the round)

Stitch marker
Tapestry needle
2 buttons for decoration

Sizing

	S	M	L
To fit head circumference (cm)	48	53	58
(in)	19	21	23
Finished size (cm)	40.5	45.75	51
(in)	16	18	20

Tension

18 sts & 24 rows = 10cm/4in over st st using 4.5mm needles

Abbreviations

See page 76.

To knit Buttoned Hat

Brim

Using 4.5mm needles, cast on 13 (15, 17) sts.

Row 1 (RS): *K1, P1; rep from * to last st, K1.

Row 2 (WS): As row 1.

Last 2 rows set moss st (US seed st). Work in moss stitch until piece measures 43.75 (49, 54) cm/ 17.25 (19.25, 21.25) in.

Cast off and break yarn.

To form the brim, bring the ends of the strip together and overlap by 3cm/1.25in. Slip-stitch the edges together on the reverse in preparation for picking up the stitches for the body of the hat.

Now, with RS of brim facing, pick up and knit 70 (80, 90) sts around the top edge. Place marker for start of round.

Body

Foundation rnd: *P9, K1; rep from * to end, rm, P1, pm.

Rnd 1: *P8, T2F; rep from * to end, rm, P1, pm.

This round sets the cable pattern for the body of the hat, and is also shown on chart A.

Repeat this round until the body of the hat, including the brim band, measures 10.75 (12, 14) cm/ 4.25 (4.75, 5.5) in.

Top

The following section is also shown on chart B.

Rnd 1: *P6, P2tog, T2F; rep from * to end, rm, P1, pm. 63 (72, 81) sts.

Rnd 2: *P7, T2F; rep from * to end, rm, P1, pm.

Rnd 3: *P5, P2tog, T2F; rep from * to end, rm, P1, pm. 56 (64, 72) sts.

Rnd 4: *P6, T2F; rep from * to end, rm, P1, pm.

Rnd 5: *P4, P2tog, T2F; rep from * to end, rm, P1, pm. 49 (56, 63) sts.

Rnd 6: *P5, T2F; rep from * to end, rm, P1, pm.

Rnd 7: *P3, P2tog, T2F; rep from * to end, rm, P1, pm. 42 (48, 54) sts.

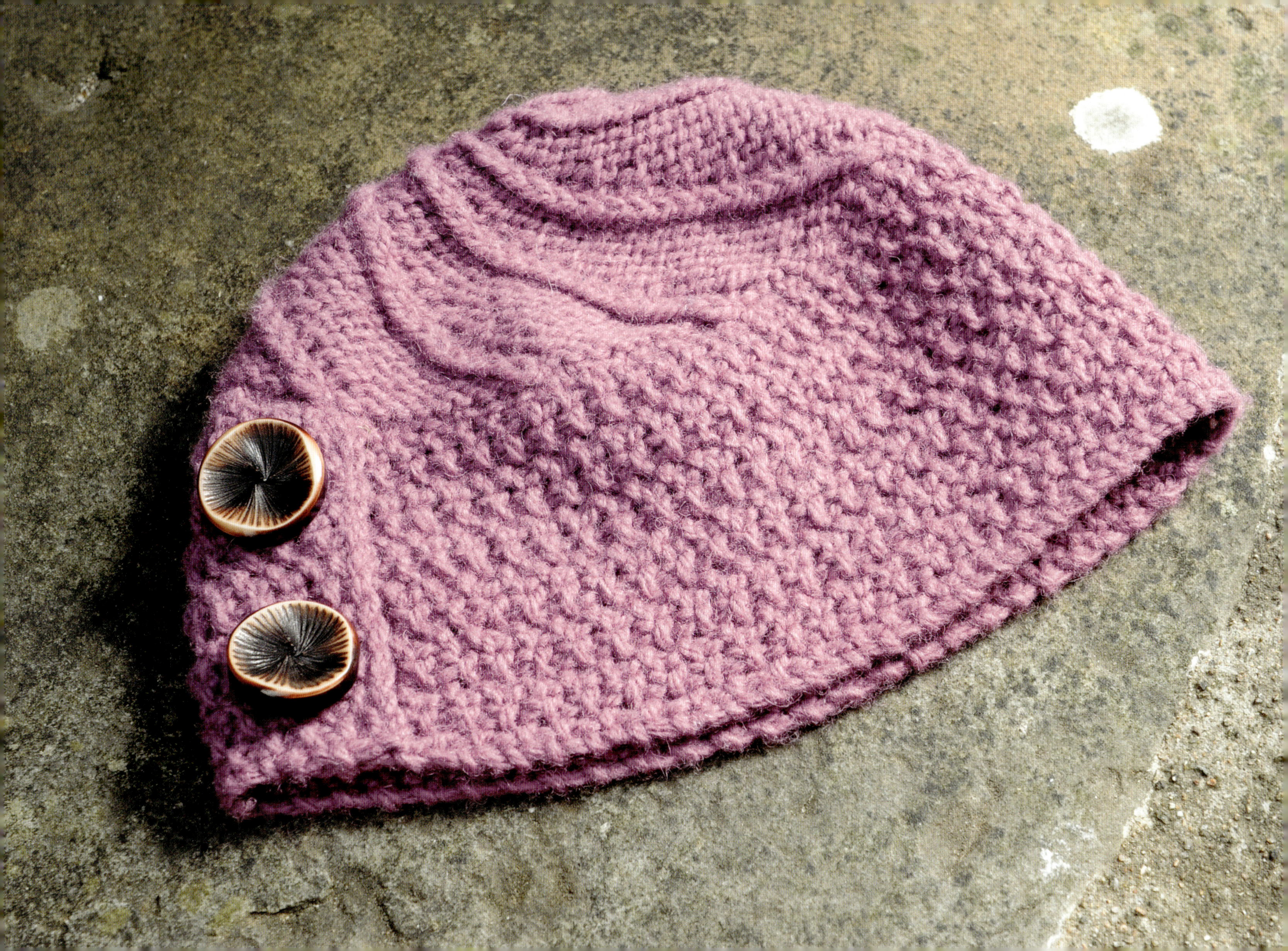

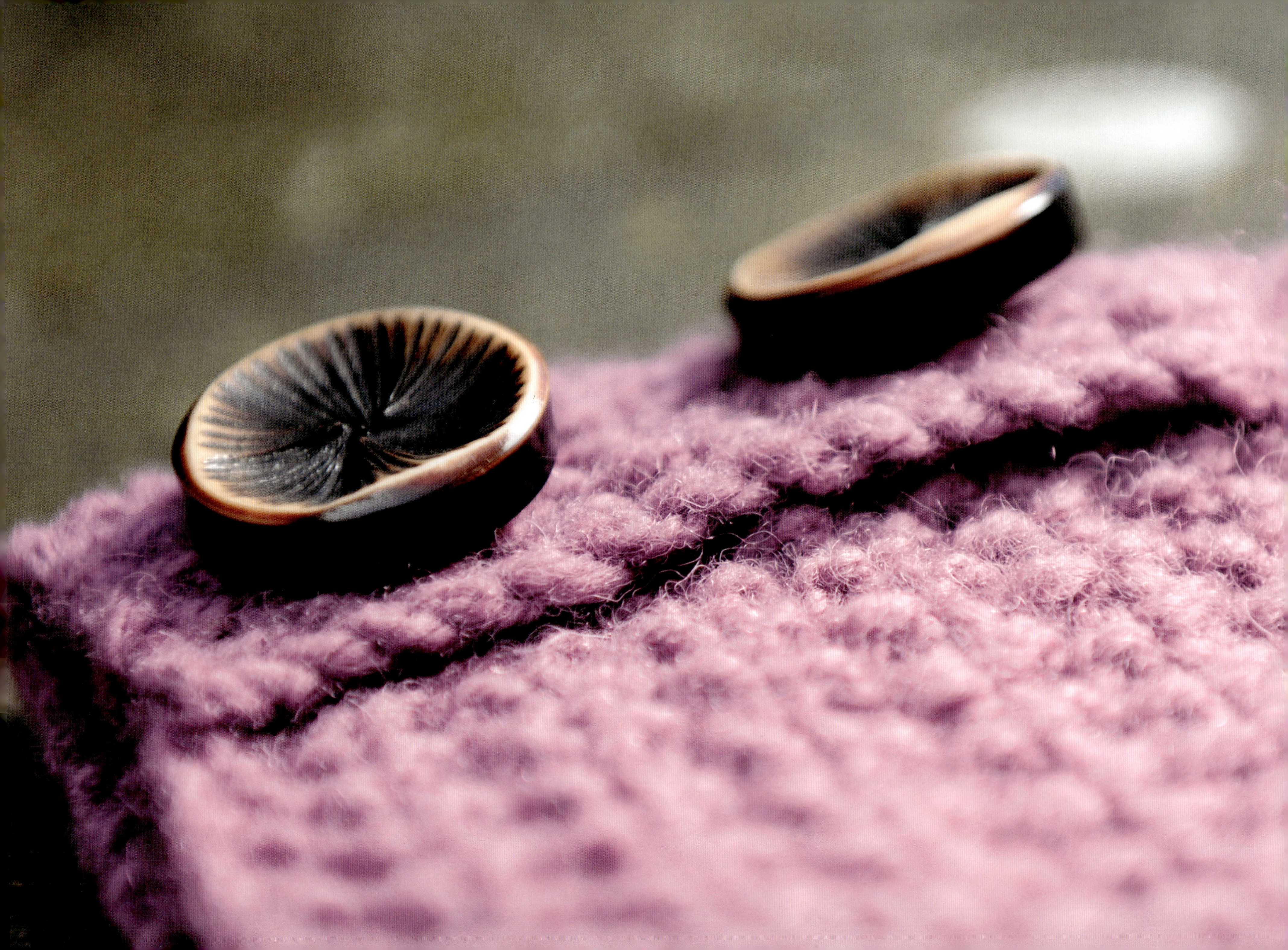

Rnd 8: *P4, T2F; rep from * to end, rm, P1, pm.

Rnd 9: *P2, P2tog, T2F; rep from * to end, rm, P1, pm. 35 (40, 45) sts.

Rnd 10: *P3, T2F; rep from * to end, rm, P1, pm.

Rnd 11: *P1, P2tog, T2F; rep from * to end, rm, P1, pm. 28 (32, 36) sts.

Rnd 12: *P2, T2F; rep from * to end, rm, P1, pm.

Rnd 13: *P2tog, T2F; rep from * to end, rm, P1, pm. 21 (24, 27) sts.

Rnd 14: *P1, SSK; rep from * to end, rm, P1, pm. 14 (16, 18) sts.

Rnd 15: *SSK; rep from * to end. 7 (8, 9) sts.

Break yarn and draw through remaining 7 (8, 9) sts, and tighten to close.

Finishing

Darn in all ends. Wash (see page 79) and block, to help the decrease lines settle in and lay flat. Sew 2 buttons to brim band for decoration.

Chart Key

- Purl on RS, Knit on WS
- SSK
- P2tog
- T2F

Chart B

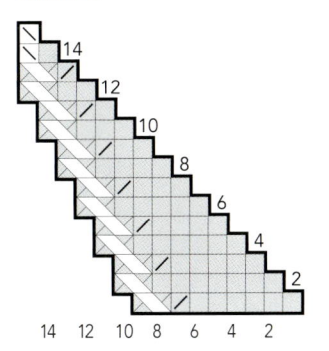

Chart A

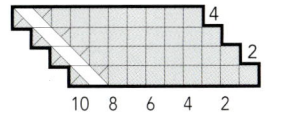

Olly's Allover
designed by Jean Moss

Materials

Jamieson & Smith Shetland Aran – 100% Real Shetland Wool (90m/50g ball)

- Yarn A – Shade BSS3: 12 (13, 13, 14, 15) x 50g balls
- Yarn B – Shade BSS14: 1 (1, 1, 2, 2) x 50g balls
- Yarn C – Shade BSS72: 1 x 50g ball
- Yarn D – Shade BSS11: 1 x 50g ball
- Yarn E – Shade BSS10: 1 x 50g ball
- Yarn F – Shade BSS2: 1 x 50g ball
- Yarn G – BSS25: 1 x 50g ball

4.5mm (UK 7/US 7) needles
5mm (UK 6/US 8) needles
4.5mm (UK 7/US 7) circular needles

Cable needle
Stitch holders
Stitch markers
Tapestry needle

Sizing

	XS	S	M	L	XL
To fit chest (cm)	96	101	106	111	116
(in)	38	40	42	44	46
Actual chest (cm)	102	107	112	117	122
(in)	40	42	44	46	48
Length to underarm (cm)	44	46.5	45	45	46.5
(in)	17.25	18.25	17.75	17.75	18.25
Actual length (cm)	68.5	71.25	71.25	71.25	73.75
(in)	27	28	28	28	29
Sleeve seam (cm)	46	46	47	47	48
(in)	18	18	18.5	18.5	19

Size shown in photograph is M (112cm/44in chest).

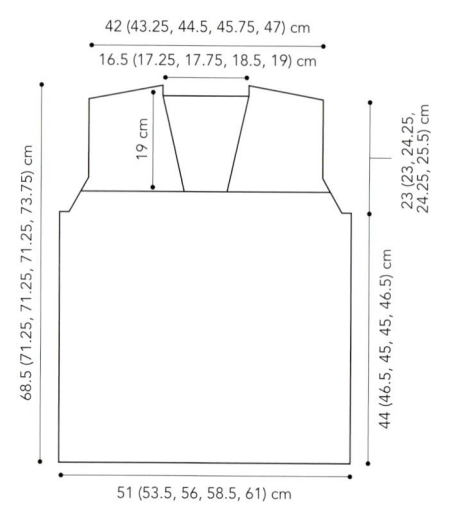

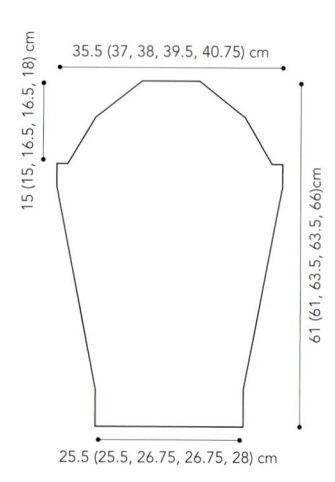

Tension

23 sts and 24 rows = 10cm/4in over Fair Isle pattern and over cable patterns using 5mm needles

Abbreviations

See page 76.

Stitch patterns

All stitch patterns are also shown on charts.

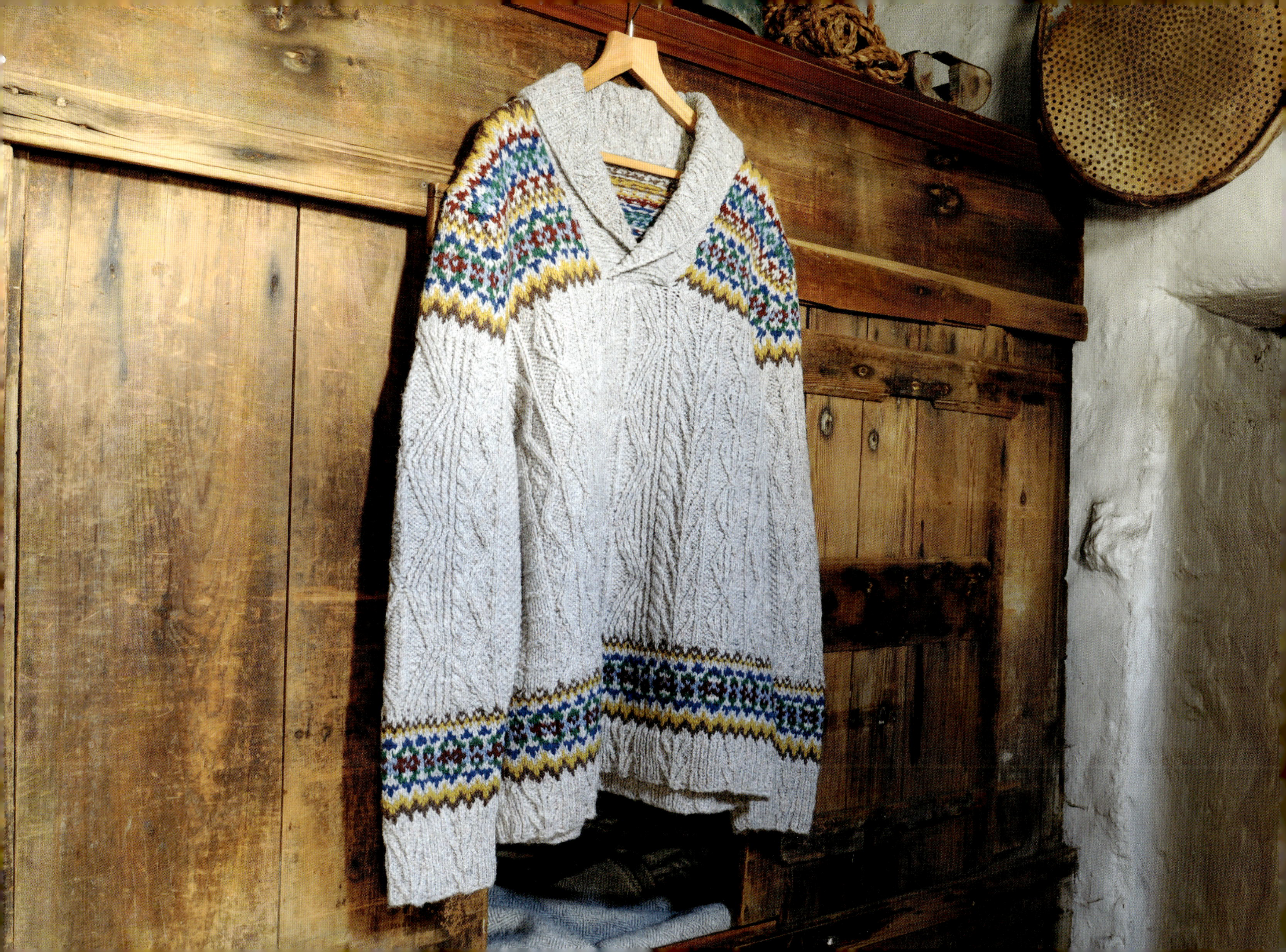

Chart A: Tree of Life
(Worked over 9 sts and 8 rows)

Row 1 (RS): P3, K3 tbl, P3.
Row 2 (WS): K3, P3 tbl, K3.
Row 3: P2, RTP, K1 tbl, LTP, P2.
Row 4: K2, (P1 tbl, K1) twice, P1 tbl, K2.
Row 5: P1, RTP, P1, K1 tbl, P1, LTP, P1.
Row 6: K1, (P1 tbl, K2) twice, P1 tbl, K1.
Row 7: RTP, P1, K3 tbl, P1, LTP.
Row 8: P1 tbl, K2, P3 tbl, K2, P1 tbl.

Chart B: Jacob's Ladder
(Worked over 7 sts and 6 rows)

Rows 1 & 3 (RS): P1, K5, P1.
Rows 2 & 4 (WS): K1, P5, K1.
Row 5: P7.
Row 6: As rows 2 & 4.

Chart C1: Zigzag & Irish Moss Stitch
(Worked over 7 sts and 20 rows)

Row 1 (RS): T3F, P4.
Row 2 and all foll WS rows: Work the stitches as they present themselves (knit the knit sts and purl the purl sts) for more detail, see chart C1.
Row 3: K1, T3F, P3.
Row 5: P1, K1, T3F, P2.
Row 7: K1, P1, K1, T3F, P1.
Row 9: (P1, K1) twice, T3F.
Row 11: (K1, P1) twice, T3B.
Row 13: P1, K1, P1, T3B, P1.
Row 15: K1, P1, T3B, P2.
Row 17: P1, T3B, P3.
Row 19: T3B, P4.
Row 20: As row 2.

Chart C2: Zigzag & Irish Moss Stitch
(Worked over 7 sts and 20 rows)

Row 1 (RS): P4, T3B.
Row 2 and all foll WS rows: Work the sts as they present themselves (knit the knit sts and purl the purl sts) for more detail, see chart C2.
Row 3: P3, T3B, K1.
Row 5: P2, T3B, K1, P1.
Row 7: P1, T3B, K1, P1, K1.
Row 9: T3B, (K1, P1) twice.
Row 11: T3F, (P1, K1) twice.
Row 13: P1, T3F, P1, K1, P1.
Row 15: P2, T3F, P1, K1.
Row 17: P3, T3F, P1.
Row 19: P4, T3F.
Row 20: As row 2.

Chart D: Aran Diamond & Twist St Rib
(Worked over 13 sts and 14 rows)

Row 1 (RS): P5, Cr3F, P5.
Row 2: K5, P3, K5.
Row 3: P4, RTP, K1 tbl, LTP, P4.
Row 4 and all foll WS rows: Work the sts as they present themselves (knit the knit sts and purl the purl sts) for more detail, see chart D.
Row 5: P3, RT, P1, K1 tbl, P1, LT, P3.
Row 7: P2, RTP, (K1 tbl, P1) twice, K1 tbl, LTP, P2.
Row 9: P2, LTP, (K1 tbl, P1) twice, K1 tbl, RTP, P2.
Row 11: P3, LTP, P1, K1 tbl, P1, RTP, P3.
Row 13: P4, LTP, P1, RTP, P4.
Row 14: K5, P1, K1, P1, K5.

Chart E: Centre Panel (Worked over 36 sts and 28 rows; Row 1 is set-up row)

Row 1 (RS): K4, P1, (K1 tbl, P1) 6 times, K2 tbl, (P1, K1 tbl) 6 times, P1, K4.
Row 2: P4, K1, (P1 tbl, K1) 6 times, P2 tbl, (K1, P1 tbl) 6 times, K1, P4.
Row 3: C4F, (P1, K1 tbl) 4 times, (RTP) 3 times, (LTP) 3 times, (K1 tbl, P1) 4 times, C4B.
Row 4: P4, K1 (P1 tbl, K1) 3 times, P2 tbl, (K1, P1 tbl) twice, K2, (P1 tbl, K1) twice, P2 tbl, (K1, P1 tbl) 3 times, K1, P4.
Row 5: K4, P1, (K1 tbl, P1) 3 times, (RTP) 3 times, Tw2, (LTP) 3 times, (P1, K1 tbl) 3 times, P1, K4.
Row 6: P4, K1, (P1 tbl, K1) 6 times, P2, (K1, P1 tbl) 6 times, K1, P4.
Row 7: C4F, (P1, K1 tbl) 3 times, (RTP) 3 times, P1, Tw2, P1, (LTP) 3 times, (K1 tbl, P1) 3 times, C4B.
Row 8: P4, (K1, P1 tbl) 3 times, (P1 tbl, K1) 3 times, K1, P2, K1, (K1, P1 tbl) 3 times, (P1 tbl, K1) 3 times, P4.
Row 9: K4, (P1, K1 tbl) twice, P1, (RTP) 3 times, P2, Tw2, P2, (LTP) 3 times, (P1, K1 tbl) twice, P1, K4.
Row 10: P4, (K1, P1 tbl) 5 times, K3, P2, K3, (P1 tbl, K1) 5 times, P4.
Row 11: C4F, (P1, K1 tbl) twice, (RTP) 3 times, P3, Tw2, P3, (LTP) 3 times, (K1 tbl, P1) twice, C4B.
Row 12: P4, (K1, P1 tbl) twice, (P1 tbl, K1) 3 times, K3, P2, K3, (K1, P1 tbl) 3 times, (P1 tbl, K1) twice, P4.
Row 13: K4, P1, K1 tbl, P1, (RTP) 3 times, P4, Tw2, P4, (LTP) 3 times, P1, K1 tbl, P1, K4.
Row 14: P4, (K1, P1 tbl) 4 times, K5, P2, K5, (P1 tbl, K1) 4 times, P4.
Row 15: C4F, P1, K1 tbl, (RTP) 3 times, P5, Tw2, P5, (LTP) 3 times, K1 tbl, P1, C4B.
Row 16: P4, K1, P2 tbl, (K1, P1 tbl) twice, K6, P2, K6, (P1 tbl, K1) twice, P2 tbl, K1, P4.
Row 17: K4, P1, (LTP) 3 times, P5, Tw2, P5, (RTP) 3 times, K1 tbl, P1, K4.
Row 18: P4, K1, (P1 tbl, K1) 4 times, K4, P2, K5, (P1 tbl, K1) 4 times, P4.
Row 19: C4F, P1, K1 tbl, P1, LTK, (LTP) twice, P4, Tw2, P4, (RTP) twice, RTK, P1, K1 tbl, P1, C4B.
Row 20: P4, (K1, P1 tbl) twice, (P1 tbl, K1) 3 times, K3, P2, K3, (K1, P1 tbl) twice, (P1 tbl, K1) twice, P4.
Row 21: K4, (P1, K1 tbl) twice, (LTP) 3 times, P3, Tw2, P3, (RTP) 3 times, (K1 tbl, P1) twice, K4.
Row 22: P4, (K1, P1 tbl) 5 times, K3, P2, K3, (P1 tbl, K1) 5 times, P4.
Row 23: C4F, (P1, K1 tbl) twice, P1, LTK, (LTP) twice, P2, Tw2, P2, (RTP) twice, RTK, (P1, K1 tbl) twice, P1, C4B.
Row 24: P4, K1 (P1 tbl, K1) twice, P2 tbl, (K1, P1 tbl) twice, K2, P2, K2, (P1 tbl, K1) twice, P2 tbl, (K1, P1 tbl) twice, K1, P4.
Row 25: K4, P1, (K1tbl, P1) twice, K1 tbl, (LTP) 3 times, P1, Tw2, P1, (RTP) 3 times, (K1 tbl, P1) 3 times, K4.
Row 26: P4, (K1, P1 tbl) 6 times, K1, P2, K1, (P1 tbl, K1) 6 times, P4.
Row 27: C4F, P1, (K1 tbl, P1) 3 times, LTK, (LTP) twice, Tw2, (RTP) twice, RTK, (P1 tbl, K1) 3 times, P1, C4B.
Row 28: P4, (K1, P1 tbl) 4 times, (P1 tbl, K1) twice, P1 tbl, P2, (K1, P1 tbl) twice, (P1 tbl, K1) 4 times, P4.
Row 29: K4, (P1, K1 tbl) 4 times, (LTP) 3 times, (RTP) 3 times, (K1 tbl, P1) 4 times, K4.

Rep rows 2–29

Moss Stitch/US Seed Stitch (Worked over an even number of stitches)

Row 1 (RS): *K1, P1; rep from * to end.
Row 2 (WS): *P1, K1; rep from * to end.

Moss Stitch/US Seed Stitch (Worked over an odd number of stitches)

Row 1 (RS): *K1, P1; rep from * to last st, K1.
Row 2 (WS): As row 1.

To knit Olly's Allover

Back

Using 4.5mm needles and yarn A, cast on 117 (123, 129, 135, 141) sts. In the following section the stitch patterns are referred to as charts, but they are given in written form as well – use whichever you would prefer.

Continue as follows:

Row 1 (RS): K0 (1, 0, 1, 0), (P1, K1) 3 (4, 2, 3, 5) times, *work 9 sts of chart A row 1, (K1, P1) 3 times, K1; rep from * to last 15 (18, 13, 16, 19) sts, work 9 sts of chart A row 1, (K1, P1) 3 (4, 2, 3, 5) times, K0 (1, 0, 1, 0).

Row 2 (WS): P0 (1, 0, 1, 0), (K1, P1) 3 (4, 2, 3, 5) times, * work 9 sts of chart A row 2, P1, (K1, P1) 3 times; rep from * to last 15 (18, 13, 16, 19) sts, work 9 sts of chart A row 2, (P1, K1) 3 (4, 2, 3, 5) times, P0 (1, 0, 1, 0).

Continue as set, working rib and chart A (tree of life), until work measures 6.5cm/2.5in, ending with RS facing for next row.

Change to 5mm needles and work from chart F as follows:

Row 1 (RS): Work sts 9 (12, 9, 12, 9) to 12 of row 1 chart F, repeat the 12 sts of the chart 9 (10, 10, 11, 11) times across row, work sts 1 to 5 (2, 5, 2, 5) of chart F.

Row 2 (WS): Work sts 5 (2, 5, 2, 5) to 1 of row 2 chart F, repeat the 12 sts of the chart 9 (10, 10, 11, 11) times across row, work sts 12 to 9 (12, 9, 12, 9) of chart F.

Work from chart F as set, until row 20 is complete.

Work row 21 of chart, substituting yarn B for yarn G.

Purl 1 row in yarn A only, then set the cable patt as foll:

XS only

Row 1 (RS): Work 8 sts in moss st, K1, work chart C1 over 7 sts, K1, work chart D over 13 sts, K1, work chart A over 9 sts, work chart E over 36 sts, work chart A over 9 sts, K1, work chart D over 13 sts, K1, work chart C2 over 7 sts, K1, work 9 sts in moss st.

Row 2 (WS): Moss st over 9 sts, P1, chart C2 over 7 sts, P1, chart D over 13 sts, P1, chart A over 9 sts, chart E over 36 sts, chart A over 9 sts, P1, chart D over 13 sts, P1, chart C1 over 7 sts, P1, moss st over 8 sts.

S, M, L & XL only

Row 1 (RS): Work 6 (9, 12, 15) sts in moss st, work chart B over 7 sts, work chart C1 over 7 sts, K1, work chart D over 13 sts, K1, work chart A over 9 sts, work chart E over 36 sts, work chart A over 9 sts, K1, work chart D over 13 sts, K1, work chart C2 over 7 sts, work chart B over 7 sts, work 5 (8, 11, 14) sts in moss st.

Row 2 (WS): Moss st over 5 (8, 11, 14) sts, chart B over 7 sts, chart C2 over 7 sts, P1, chart D over 13 sts, P1, chart A over 9 sts, chart E over 36 sts, chart A over 9 sts, P1, chart D over 13 sts, P1, chart C1 over 7 sts, chart B over 7 sts, moss st over 6 (9, 12, 15) sts.

All sizes

Last 2 rows set cable patterns. Cont as set, keeping all patterns correct until work measures 44 (46.5, 45, 45, 46.5) cm/ 17.25 (18.25, 17.75, 7.75, 18.25) in from cast-on edge, ending with RS facing for next row.

Armhole shaping

Keeping patterns correct, cast off 6 (6, 7, 7, 7) sts at beg of next 2 rows. 105 (111, 115, 121, 127) sts.

Dec 1 st at both ends of next and 4 (5, 6, 7, 9) foll alt rows. 95 (99, 101, 105, 107) sts.†

Work 1 more row in patt, thus ending with RS facing for next row.

Work from chart F as foll:

Row 1 (RS): Work sts 8 (12, 11, 9, 8) to 12 of row 1 chart F, repeat the 12 sts of chart 7 (8, 8, 8, 8) times across row, work sts 1 to 6 (2, 3, 5, 6) sts of chart F.

Row 2 (WS): Work sts 6 (2, 3, 5, 6) to 1 of row 2 chart F, repeat the 12 sts of chart 7 (8, 8, 8, 8) times across row, work sts 12 to 8 (12, 11, 9, 8) of chart F.

Cont in patt as set by last 2 rows until work measures 66.75 (69.25, 69.25, 69.25, 71.75)cm/ 26.25 (27.25, 27.25, 27.25, 28.25) in from cast-on edge, ending with RS facing for next row.

Shoulder and neck shaping

Note: When the 38 rows of chart F are completed, work to end of yoke in st st using yarn A only.

Keeping patterns correct, place 9 (10, 10, 10, 10) sts at armhole edge on a stitch holder at start of next 2 rows.

Next row (RS): Place 10 (10, 10, 11, 11) sts at armhole edge on holder, work 11 (11, 11, 12, 12) sts in patt as set, cast off 35 (37, 39, 39, 41) sts for neck and place rem sts on a holder.

Re-join new yarn to rem right shoulder sts and cont as foll:

Next row (WS): Work in patt as set, dec 1 st at neck edge.

Next row (RS): Place all right shoulder sts (from holders) on one needle and cast off over all 29 (30, 30, 32, 32) sts.

Work the left shoulder to match, reversing shapings.

Front

Work as for Back to † .

Neck Shaping

Next row (WS): Working from chart as set, work 36 (38, 39, 41, 42) sts and place these on a holder, then cast off 23 sts and work to end in pattern. 36 (38, 39, 41, 42) sts.

Work from chart F as foll:

Row 1 (RS): Work sts 8 (12, 11, 9, 8) to 12 of row 1 chart F, repeat the 12 sts of chart 2 (3, 3, 3, 3) times across row, work sts 1 to 7 (1, 1, 1, 1) of chart F.

Row 2 (WS): Work sts 7 (1, 1, 1, 1) to 1 of row 2 chart F, repeat the 12 sts of chart 2 (3, 3, 3, 3) times across row, work sts 12 to 8 (12, 11, 9, 8) of chart F.

Working in chart F pattern as set, dec as follows:

Dec 1 st at neck edge on next and 6 (7, 8, 8, 9) foll 6th (5th, 4th, 4th, 4th) rows. 29 (30, 30, 32, 32) sts.

Cont in patt as set until work measures 66.75 (69.25, 69.25, 69.25, 71.75) cm/26.25 (27.25, 27.25, 27.25, 28.25) in from cast-on edge, ending with RS facing for next row.

Note: When the 38 rows of chart F are completed, work to end of yoke in st st using yarn A only.

Shape shoulder

Place 9 (10, 10, 10, 10) sts at armhole edge on holder, work to end. Work 1 row.

Place 10 (10, 10, 11, 11) sts at armhole edge on holder, work to end. Work 1 row.

Place all shoulder sts on one needle and cast off over all 29 (30, 30, 32, 32) sts.

With RS facing, re-join yarn to sts on hold for right shoulder. 36 (38, 39, 41, 42) sts.

Work from chart F as foll:

Row 1 (RS): Work sts 6 (12, 12, 12, 12) to 12 of row 1 chart F, repeat the 12 sts of chart 2 (3, 3, 3, 3) times across row, work sts 1 to 5 (1, 2, 4, 5) sts of chart.

Row 2 (WS): Work sts 5 (1, 2, 4, 5) to 1 of row 2 chart F, repeat the 12 sts of chart 2 (3, 3, 3, 3) times across row, work sts 12 to 6 (12, 12, 12, 12) sts of chart.

Complete right shoulder to match left, reversing shapings.

Sleeves

Using 4.5mm needles and yarn A, cast on 59 (59, 61, 61, 63) sts and cont as foll:

Row 1 (RS): P0 (0, 1, 1, 0), (K1, P1) 1 (1, 1, 1, 2) times, *(K1, P1) 3 times, K1, work 9 sts of chart A; rep from * 2 more times, (K1, P1) 4 (4, 5, 5, 5) times, K1 (1, 0, 0, 1).

Row 2 (WS): P1 (1, 0, 0, 1), (K1, P1) 4 (4, 5, 5, 5) times, *work 9 sts of chart A, P1, (K1, P1) 3 times; rep from * 2 more times, (K1, P1) 1 (1, 1, 1, 2) times, K0 (0, 1, 1, 0).

Cont as set, working the rib and tree of life pattern until the work measures 9cm/3.5in, ending with RS facing for next row.

Change to 5mm needles and work from chart F as foll:

Row 1 (RS): Work sts 8 (8, 0, 0, 12) to 12 (12, 0, 0, 12) of row 1 chart F, repeat the 12 sts of chart 4 (4, 5, 5, 5) times across row, work sts 1 to 6 (6, 1, 1, 2) of chart F.

Row 2 (WS): Work sts 6 (6, 1, 1, 2) to 1 of row 2 chart F, repeat the 12 sts of chart 4 (4, 5, 5, 5) times across row, work sts 12 to 8 (8, 0, 0, 12) of chart F.

Work from chart F as set until chart row 20 is complete, and **at the same time** inc 1 st at both ends of 8th (6th, 6th, 5th, 5th) chart row and on 10 (11, 12, 13, 14) foll 7th (7th, 7th, 6th, 6th) rows. 81 (83, 87, 89, 93) sts.

Cont to work shaping as set, and work row 21 of chart, but substitute yarn B for yarn G.

Purl 1 row using yarn A only.

When chart F rows are complete, cont to inc in cable patt as follows:

Sizes XS, S & M only

Row 1 (RS): Moss st over 6 (6, 7) sts, K1, chart C1 over 7 sts, chart E over 36 sts, chart C2 over 7 sts, K1, moss st over 7 (7, 8) sts.

Row 2 (WS): Moss st over 7 (7, 8) sts, P1, chart C2 over 7 sts, chart E over 36 sts, chart C1 over 7 sts, P1, moss st over 6 (6, 7) sts.

Sizes L & XL only

Row 1 (RS): Inc in first st, moss st over (7, 8) sts, K1, chart C1 over 7 sts, chart E over 36 sts, chart C2 over 7 sts, K1, moss st over (6, 7) sts, inc in last st. (69, 71) sts.

Row 2 (WS): Moss st over (8, 9) sts, P1, chart C2 over 7 sts, chart E over 36 sts, chart C1 over 7 sts, P1, moss st over (9, 10) sts.

All sizes

Cont in patt as set, working the inc sts in moss st. When incs are completed, cont in patt until work measures 46 (46, 47, 47, 48) cm/18 (18, 18.5, 18.5, 19) in from cast-on edge ending with RS facing for next row. 81 (83, 87, 89, 93) sts.

Shape sleevehead

Keeping patterns correct, cast off 6 (6, 7, 7, 7) sts at beg of next 2 rows. 69 (71, 73, 75, 79) sts.

Keeping patts correct, dec 1 st at both ends of next 6 (8, 6, 6, 8) rows, then on next 12 (11, 14, 14, 14) alt rows. 33 (33, 33, 35, 35) sts.

At the same time after 9 (9, 13, 13, 15) rows rows of decs have been worked, purl 1 row in yarn A, then refer to chart F and starting on row 1, work in Fair Isle to end, keeping decs and patt correct as set.

When all decs have been worked, work 1 row without shaping.

Cast off 3 sts at beg of next 4 rows.

Cast off rem 21 (21, 21, 23, 23) sts.

Finishing

Use a small neat backstitch on edge of work for all seams except ribs, where a slip-stitch should be used. Join shoulder seams.

Collar

Using 5mm needles and yarn A, loosely cast on 145 (147, 149, 151, 153) sts.

Change to 4.5mm needles and work as foll:

Row 1 (RS): K0 (1, 0, 1, 0), (P1, K1) 2 (2, 3, 3, 4) times, *work 9 sts of chart A, (K1, P1) 3 times, K1; rep from * 7 more times, work 9 sts of chart A, (K1, P1) 2 (2, 3, 3, 4) times, K0 (1, 0, 1, 0).

Row 2 (WS): P0 (1, 0, 1, 0), (K1, P1) 2 (2, 3, 3, 4) times, *work 9 sts of chart A, (P1, K1) 3 times, P1; rep from * 7 more times, work 9 sts of chart A, (P1, K1) 2 (2, 3, 3, 4) times, P0 (1, 0, 1, 0).

Last 2 rows set chart pattern and rib, cont to work as set until piece meas 10cm/4in from cast-on edge, ending with RS facing for next row.

Keeping patterns correct, cast off 4 sts at beg of next 21 rows. 61 (63, 65, 67, 69) sts.

Work 1 row in patt then cast off loosely using 5mm needles.

Placing right side of sweater to wrong side of collar, attach collar using neat slip-stitch as foll:

Starting at right front neck edge, sew side edge (10cm/4in) of collar along horizontal edge at bottom of neck. Sew sloping edge of collar to sloping edge of left front neck, sew cast off edge to straight edge at top of left front neck, across back neck and down straight edge at right front neck, then sew other sloping edge to sloping edge of right front neck. Finally, sew side edge of collar along horizontal edge behind the first one, ending at left front neck edge.

Insert sleeves, making sure Fair Isle matches up as far as you can, with no puckering across top of armhole. Join side and sleeve seams in one line, matching ribs and Fair Isle bands.

Chart Key

- Knit on RS, Purl on WS
- Purl on RS, Knit on WS
- K1 tbl on RS, P1 tbl on WS
- RTP
- LTP
- LTK
- RTK
- RT
- LT
- Cr3F
- Tw2
- CB4
- CF4
- T3F
- T3B

- Yarn A (BSS3); Knit on RS, Purl on WS
- Yarn B (BSS14); Knit on RS, Purl on WS
- Yarn C (BSS72); Knit on RS, Purl on WS
- Yarn D (BSS11); Knit on RS, Purl on WS
- Yarn E (BSS10); Knit on RS, Purl on WS
- Yarn F (BSS2); Knit on RS, Purl on WS
- Yarn G (BSS25); Knit on RS, Purl on WS

Chart A: Tree of Life

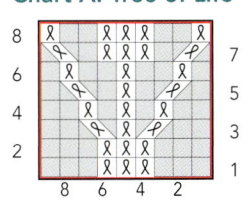

Chart B: Jacob's Ladder

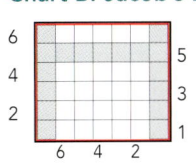

Chart F (Fair Isle Pattern)

Chart C1: Zigzag & Irish Moss Stitch

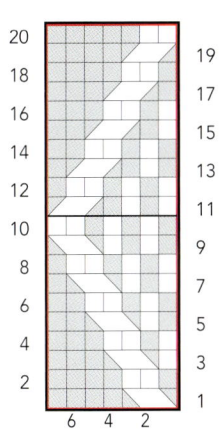

Chart C2: Zigzag & Irish Moss Stitch

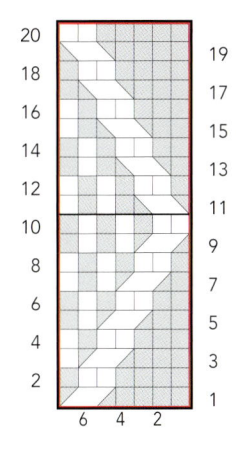

Chart D: Aran Diamond & Twist St Rib

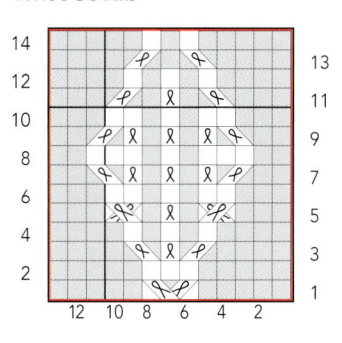

Chart E: Centre Panel

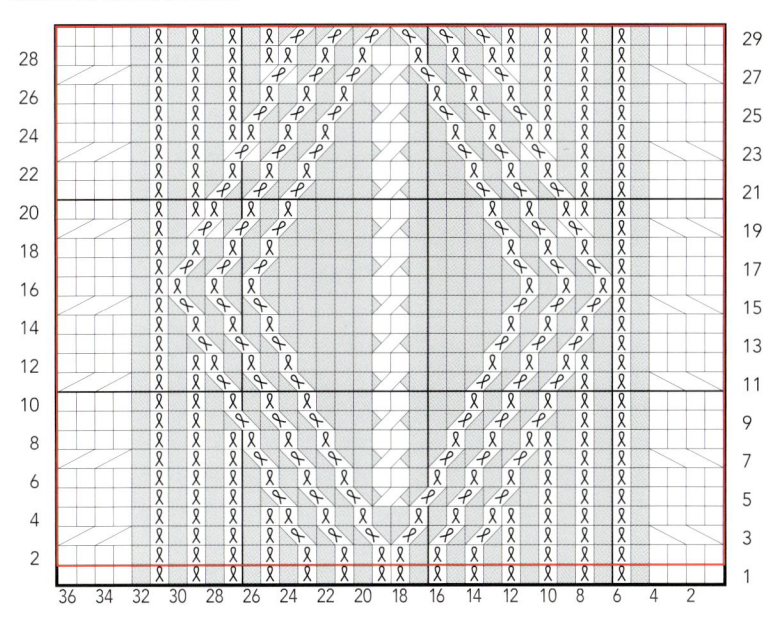

Abbreviations

C4B	Slip next 2 sts to cable needle and hold at back, K2, then K2 from cable needle
C4F	Slip next 2 sts to cable needle and hold at front, K2, then K2 from cable needle
cm	Centimetre(s)
cont	Continue(s)/continuing
Cr3F	Slip next 2 sts to cable needle and hold at front, K1 tbl, then P1, K1 tbl from cable needle
dec(s)	Decrease(s)/decreasing
DPN(s)	Double-pointed needle(s)
foll	Follows/following
g	Grams
in	Inch(es)
inc(s)	Increase(s)/increasing
K	Knit
K1A(B/C/D/E)	Knit 1 stitch using yarn A(B/C/D/E) as indicated.
K2(3)tog	Knit the next 2(3) stitches together
K2togE	Knit together one edging stitch with one stitch from main part of shawl
KFB	Knit into front and back of same stitch. Increases 1 stitch.
LT	Slip next st to cable needle and hold at front, K1 tbl then K1 tbl from cable needle
LTK	Slip next st to cable needle and hold at front, K1, then K1 tbl from cable needle
LTP	Sl next stitch to cable needle and hold at front, P1 then K1 tbl from cable needle
M1	Make 1. Worked as M1L.
M1L	Make 1 Left. Using left-hand needle, pick up the strand between stitches from front to back and knit through the back of this loop.
M1R	Make 1 Right. Using left-hand needle, pick up the strand between stitches from back to front and knit this loop.
MB	Make Bobble. (K1, P1, K1) all into next stitch. Turn. P3. Turn. Sl 1, K2tog, psso.
meas	Measures/measuring
mm	Millimetre
P	Purl
P1A(B/C/D/E)	Purl 1 stitch using yarn A(B/C/D/E) as indicated
P2tog	Purl the next 2 sts together
patt(s)	Pattern(s)
PFB	Purl into front and back of same stitch
pm	Place marker
psso	Pass slipped stitch(es) over
rem	Remain(s)/remaining
rep	Repeat
rm	Remove stitch marker from its current position
Rnd	Round
RS	Right side
RT	Slip next stitch to cable needle and hold at back, K1 tbl then K1 tbl from cable needle
RTK	Slip next stitch to cable needle and hold at back, K1 tbl, then K1 from cable needle
RTP	Slip next stitch to cable needle and hold at back, K1 tbl, then P1 from cable needle
s2kpo	Slip 2 stitches knitwise together, as if to K2tog but do not knit them together. Knit the next stitch on the left-hand needle and pass the two slipped stitches over. This creates a centred double decrease. 2 sts decreased.
Sl 1	Slip 1 stitch from left-hand to right-hand needle without twisting (purlwise)
slm	Slip marker from left-hand to right-hand needle.
SSK	Slip next 2 sts separately knitwise to right-hand needle, then place tip of left needle through the front of these 2 stitches and knit them together. This creates a left-leaning decrease. 1 st decreased.
st st	Stocking stitch (US: stockinette stitch)
st(s)	Stitch(es)
T2F	Slip next stitch onto cable needle and hold at front of work, P1; K1 from the cable needle
T3B	Slip next stitch to cable needle and hold at back, K2, then P1 from cable needle
T3F	Slip next 2 stitches to cable needle and hold at front, P1, then K2 from cable needle
tbl	Through the back loop
Tw2	Knit second stitch on left-hand needle, then knit first stitch and slip both loops off together
w&t	Wrap and turn. Take yarn to opposite side of work (if knitting, take to front and if purling take yarn to back), slip next st purlwise to right-hand needle, return yarn to working side, slip stitch back to left-hand needle. Turn work without working the remaining stitches in the row.
WS	Wrong side
yo	Yarnover

Project Gallery

Wave Cardigan — page 10

Feathercrest Mittens — page 16

Peat Hill Waistcoat — page 20

Cross Tam — page 26

Viking Tunic — page 30

Osaka Tea Cosy — page 34

Kergord Scarf — page 38

Melby Jumper Dress — page 42

Wool Brokers Socks — page 46

Muckleberry Gloves & Hat — page 50

Caavie Gansey — page 54

Madeira Lace Shawl — page 60

Buttoned Hat — page 66

Olly's Allover — page 70

Designers

Jared Flood is a New York-based knitwear designer and photographer. One of the best known names in contemporary knitting, Jared holds an MFA from the New York Academy of Art, and travels America teaching traditional hand-knitting techniques and garment construction. His designs have featured in *Interweave Knits*, *Vogue Knitting* and *Knit.1*; and his photographs in *Good Housekeeping*, *New York Magazine*, *NY Spaces*, *NY Living* and *Vogue Knitting*. Jared recently launched his own line of yarns, Shelter.

Daniel Goldman is a knitwear designer and musician living in Sweden. He studies techniques and teaches hand-knitting from his Stockholm workshop. His interest in the history of the craft, as well as aspects of traditional and ethnic knitting styles, and fibre colour theory, has led to a research based approach to developing designs and techniques. Daniel is currently working on a collection of advanced knitting techniques.

Gudrun Johnston was born in Shetland while her mother was running knitwear design company, The Shetland Trader. Gudrun's history with Shetland wool, which she strives to include in her designs, began at birth when she was wrapped in traditional hap shawls. Some thirty years later—having lived in the United States and returned to Scotland—Gudrun has followed in her mother's footsteps. Under the revived name of The Shetland Trader, Gudrun issues her internationally celebrated designs and recently published her first book of hand-knit designs, *The Shetland Trader: Book One*.

Mary Kay was born and grew up in Lerwick as part of a generation that learned to knit as bairns. Mary knitted both openwork and Fair Isle until she learned to spin. Then she became utterly hooked on Shetland Fine Lace and the process of designing and putting motifs together with her own hand-spun yarn. She was one of the first designers to produce patterns for national knitting magazines, and has a long friendship with Jamieson & Smith. Mary lives in the centre of Lerwick, where she continues to knit, spin, design and pass on her skills.

Sandra Manson has lived her whole life in Shetland, where she now works for Jamieson & Smith with her assistant, Toby the Yorkshire Terrier. Her granny taught her to knit from the age of four. Sandra sold her first pair of mittens to a Lerwick hosiery merchant as a child and still works to commission for clients all over the world. In 2010 her garments were shown at London Fashion Week as part of a Lu Flux/Jamieson & Smith collaboration.

Jean Moss has worked with Shetland yarn ever since her earliest days as a hand-knit designer for Ralph Lauren. Her designs combine texture, colour and classic styling. Olly's Allover is a good example of Jean's handprint, adapted from one of her designs for Polo Ralph Lauren. Jean now tours the UK and abroad passing on her incredible design skills through classes.

Mary Jane Mucklestone has a BFA in printmaking from the Pratt Institute in Brooklyn. She also studied fashion at Parson's School of Design in Manhattan, and textiles at the University of Washington. Mary Jane has worked as a photo-stylist for *Interweave Knits* magazine, taught handwork in a Waldorf school, and had many fashion jobs in New York City, including painting silk for Oscar del la Renta. Now a renowned hand-knit designer, Mary Jane lives in Searsmont, Maine, and has travelled to Peru and Shetland to learn more about colourwork in knitting.

Hazel Tindall was taught to knit as an infant, and went on to become the world's fastest knitter in 2008. Hazel's speciality is in Fair Isle: she knitted her first all-over while still at primary school in Shetland and her teenage years were spent learning about colours and patterns by knitting Fair Isle yokes. She still uses her first charted motifs, carefully selecting them to fit the size and shape of her garment designs, using Real Shetland Wool for its lightness, warmth and ability to create sculpted shapes. Hazel's ambition is to pass on her skills to a younger generation.

Toshiyuki Shimada lives and works in Toyko, Japan. He has published several books which have been translated into multiple languages, and has had countless designs in *Vogue Nippon*. Toshi is a master of his craft and creates perfectly constructed, seamless garments with an exceptionally high level of attention to detail and symmetry. His designs use Real Shetland Wool in ways that best combine technique and colour, and apply knitting methods developed through the Isles' long history with knitting. The collaboration with Grace Williamson for Knit Real Shetland brings out the best of the designer and engineer in both individuals.

Lesley Smith was born and brought up in a family of knitters on the isle of Burra in Shetland. Her interest in knitwear began when she studied textiles at Glasgow School of Art. Returning home led her to experiment with machine knitting and progress to a career as an outworker, freelance designer and tutor. Lesley then went on to work at Jamieson & Smith for many years. Influenced by customers, her co-worker Joyce Ward and the yarn, she started hand-knitting and never stopped. Lesley is now a designer-maker, best known for her beautiful socks.

Candace Eisner Strick is based in New England, USA. Since retiring from 16 years of teaching cello, she has taught knitting all over the world and published several books on the craft. Candace's designs have been featured in numerous magazines. Together with her husband, she now runs her own yarn and knitwear company.

Joyce Ward is from Lerwick. She was taught to knit during her early years, and developed her skills throughout her childhood and teens before going on to study textiles at the Shetland College. Joyce then started her own business and later worked for Jamieson & Smith. During her time with the company, she spent more time knitting, and learned to spin through contact with customers, the encouragement of Oliver Henry and the knowledge and skills of Mary Kay. For Joyce, knitting with Real Shetland Wool has been many things: exciting, inspiring, a source of income, and a way to meet new people and keep up with old friends.

Grace Williamson lives on the isle of Burra in Shetland, where she has a knitting and wool studio, and a flock of Shetland Sheep. She works with Jamieson & Smith on a regular basis, test-knitting and applying her eye for perfection, symmetry and meticulous attention to detail to patterns and designs. Working with Toshiyuki Shimada's design, Grace developed the construction and colour flow of the Wave Cardigan in a collaboration that defines Knit Real Shetland and Jamieson & Smith.

Woolly Wormhead was taught to knit at the age of 3 before going on to study the science of dyeing and textile production at Bolton University and textiles at Goldsmith's College, University of London. Woolly is a qualified art and textile teacher, which brings a different perspective to her craft, and encourages experimentation and development in her own work. She specialises in hats because of their form, shape functionality and ability to express personality and individuality. She recently published her fourth book, *Bambeanies*.

Masami Yokoyama grew up in Osaka, Japan, and now lives in London. Inspired by her grandmother, who knitted quickly and beautifully, and by Jamieson & Smith yarn, Masami started experimenting with Fair Isle knitting. She loves the touch, colours and properties of lightness and warmth of Real Shetland Wool. Masami is inspired and amazed by the endless colour combinations and the unique techniques developed through the centuries of Shetland knitting.

Kate Davies is a designer, writer and textile historian. She has produced written and photographic pieces for *Selvedge* and *The Knitter*, and recently launched her own digital magazine, *Textisles*. Her website is archived by the British Library to preserve UK documentary heritage. Kate has visited Shetland on several occasions to research the Isles' connections with wool and knitting. Kate often uses Real Shetland Wool in her designs, which are inspired by the culture, heritage and landscape of the English North, Scotland and Shetland.

General Information

Tension

It is important to check your tension before starting a project. Tension, also known as gauge, is the number of stitches and rows in a given length, usually 10cm/4in. This determines the measurements of a garment, so getting your tension right before starting is crucial.

Take a minute to knit a swatch, about 15cm/6in square, then wash and pin it out in the same way you would the final garment. Count the number of stitches and rows across the central 10cm. If the number of stitches and rows is more than that in the pattern, your tension is high. Changing to larger needles will help correct the problem. If the number of stitches is fewer than specified then your tension is low and you will need to switch to smaller needles. It helps to remember that your tension can vary with your mood, when working back and forth versus in the round, and that it can be slightly different when working over a large number of stitches in the actual garment.

Washing and finishing

To wash, put some wool wash or soap flakes in lukewarm (cosy, but never hot) water and gently immerse. Carefully lift out the piece and repeat in the same temperature of water, this time without the soap. Repeat this with fresh water until all the soap is gone.

Gently squeeze the water out, making sure not to wring the garment, and then roll in a clean, dry towel until most of the water is removed. To dry, lay or pin your garment to the measurements necessary, following any specific finishing instructions for your piece.

After washing and finishing your garment is ready for wearing or gifting, and should last a lifetime. Shetland knits are passed down through generations, with arms and necklines re-knitted and delicate lace repaired and carefully conserved. Storing your wool and garments with a sprig of lavender will help keep moths away and your beautiful Real Shetland Wool looking its best for decades.

Knitting techniques

The patterns in this collection use a range of special knitting techniques, including different cast-on methods, colourwork techniques and stitch patterns. You will find detailed directions on each of these methods in many knitting reference books, as well as through the wide range of online tutorial resources.

Acknowledgements

Thank you to Oliver Henry for his idea to produce this book, and for everything; Martin Curtis for his encouragement and good advice; Sandra Manson for being a trusted second pair of eyes; Derek Goudie for his calmness and clarity of thought on the tough bits; June Moulder for all her help; Louise Birnie and Stuart Hughes for their comments during the final stages; Grace Williamson for her advice and honest opinions, and her knitting; Jen Arnall-Culliford for technical editing and for making the hard bits easy; Dave Donaldson for his beautiful photos and dry humour; Shetland Amenity Trust for kindly letting us shoot the photographs at the Crofthouse Museum; Deborah Leggate and Misa Hay at Promote Shetland for helping with contacts; Jordan Ogg for copy editing, and Sarah Dearlove for casting an eye over the collection at a crucial stage.

Most of all thanks to Laura Palumbo for the beautiful graphics, layouts and charts; advice and patience; being around to bounce ideas with from start to finish; all the extremely hard work, late nights and long weekends, and for making us both giggle. This book wouldn't have happened without her.

—*Sarah Laurenson*
Editor